Jeanette Winterson

Sonya Andermahr

First published 2009 by
PALGRAVE MACMILLAN

Palgrave Macmillan in the UK is an imprint of Macmillan Publishers Limited
registered in England, company number 785998, of Houndmills, Basingstoke
Hampshire RG21 6XS.

Palgrave Macmillan in the US is a division of St Martin's Press LLC,
175 Fifth Avenue, New York, NY 10010.

Palgrave Macmillan is the global academic imprint of the above companies
and has companies and representatives throughout the world.

Palgrave® and Macmillan® are registered trademarks in the United States,
the United Kingdom, Europe and other countries.

ISBN-13: 978–0–230–50760–9 hardback
ISBN-10: 0–230–50760–3 hardback
ISBN-13: 978–0–230–50761–6 paperback
ISBN-10: 0–230–50761–1 paperback

This book is printed on paper suitable for recycling and made from fully
managed and sustained forest sources. Logging, pulping and manufacturing
processes are expected to conform to the environmental regulations of the
country of origin.

A catalogue record for this book is available from the British Library.

Library of Congress Cataloging-in-Publication Data
Andermahr, Sonya.
    Jeanette Winterson / Sonya Andermahr.
        p.   cm. — (New British fiction)
    Includes bibliographical references and index.
    ISBN-13: 978–0–230–50760–9 (hbk.)
    ISBN-10: 0–230–50760–3 (hbk.)
    ISBN-13: 978–0–230–50761–6 (pbk.)
    ISBN-10: 0–230–50761–1 (pbk.)
        1. Winterson, Jeanette, 1959—Criticism and interpretation.   I. Title.
    PR6073.I558Z58 2009
    823'.914—dc22   2008037811

10   9   8   7   6   5   4   3   2   1
18   17   16   15   14   13   12   11   10   09

Printed and bound in China

NEW BRITISH FICTION

Series editors:

Philip Tew
Rod Mengham

Published
Sonya Andermahr: **Jeanette Winterson**
Bradley Buchanan: **Hanif Kureishi**
Frederick M. Holmes: **Julian Barnes**
Kaye Mitchell: **A.L. Kennedy**
Robert Morace: **Irvine Welsh**
Stephen Morton: **Salman Rushdie**

Forthcoming
Rod Mengham: **Jonathan Coe**
Mark Rawlinson: **Pat Barker**
Philip Tew: **Zadie Smith**
Lynn Wells: **Ian McEwan**
Wendy Wheeler: **A.S. Byatt**

New British Fiction Series
Series Standing Order

ISBN 1–4039–4274–9 hardback
ISBN 1–4039–4275–7 paperback
(*outside North America only*)

You can receive future titles in this series as they are published by placing a standing order. Please contact your bookseller or, in the case of difficulty, write to us at the address below with your name and address, the title of the series and the ISBN quoted above.

Customer Services Department, Palgrave Ltd
Houndmills, Basingstoke, Hampshire RG21 6XS, England

CONTENTS

GENERAL EDITORS' PREFACE

This series highlights with its very title two crucial elements in the nature of contemporary British fiction, especially as a field for academic research and study. The first term indicates the originality and freshness of such writing expressed in a huge formal diversity. The second evokes the cultural identity of the authors included, who nevertheless represent through their diversity a challenge to any hegemonic or narrow view of Britishness. As regards the fiction, many of the writers featured in this series continue to draw from and adapt long traditions of cultural and aesthetic practice. Such aesthetic continuities contrast starkly with the conditions of knowledge at the end of the twentieth century and the beginning of the twenty-first, a period that has been characterized by an apprehension of radical presentness, a sense of unprecedented forms of experience and an obsession with new modes of self-awareness. This stage of the survival of the novel may perhaps be best remembered as a millennial and post-millennial moment, a time of fluctuating reading practices and of historical events whose impact is largely still unresolved. The new fiction of these times reflects a rapidly changing cultural and ideological reality, as well as a renewal of the commitment of both writers and readers to both the relevance and utility of narrative forms of knowledge.

Each volume in this series will serve as an introductory guide to an individual author chosen from a list of those whose work has proved to be of general interest to reviewers, academics, students and the general reading public. Each volume will offer information concerning the life, work and literary and cultural contexts appropriate to the chosen subject of each book; individual volumes will share the same overall structure with a largely common organization of materials. The result is intended to be suitable for both academic and general readers: putting accessibility at a premium, without compromising an ambitious series of readings of today's most vitally interesting British novelists, interpreting their work, assessing their influences, and exploring their relationship to the times in which they live.

Philip Tew and Rod Mengham

ACKNOWLEDGEMENTS

I owe thanks to a number of people who have helped me in the writing of this book: Jeanette Winterson for agreeing to a short interview; Phil Tew for his help and advice at the start and end of the project; Kate Haines, Kitty Van Boxel and Sonya Barker at Palgrave Macmillan for their patient support. Thanks also to the anonymous reader for their positive feedback. Finally, I would like to thank my mum, Jill Scott-Lee, for her encouragement.

LIST OF ABBREVIATIONS

AL – *Art & Lies: A Piece for Three Voices and a Bawd*
AO – *Art Objects: Essays on Ecstasy and Effrontery*
GS – *Gut Symmetries*
KC – *The King of Capri*
L – *Lighthousekeeping*
O – *Oranges*
P – *Passion*
PB – *The PowerBook*
S – *Sexing the Cherry*
SG – *The Stone Gods*
T – *Tanglewreck*
W – *Weight*
WB – *Written on the Body*
WP – *The World and Other Places*

PART I
Introduction

TIMELINE

1960   Harold Macmillan 'Winds of Change' speech, Cape
Town, South Africa
John F. Kennedy elected as US President
Aged six, Kazuo Ishiguro arrives in Britain

1961   Adolf Eichmann on trial in Israel for role in Holocaust
Bay of Pigs: attempted invasion of Cuba
Berlin Wall constructed
Yuri Gagarin first person in space
Silicon chip patented
Private Eye magazine begins publication
Muriel Spark, *The Prime of Miss Jean Brodie*
Jonathan Coe born

1962   Cuban Missile Crisis
Marilyn Monroe dies
Independence for Uganda; followed this decade by
Kenya (1963), Northern Rhodesia (1964), Southern
Rhodesia (1965), Barbados (1966)

1963   John F. Kennedy assassinated in Dallas
Martin Luther King Jr delivers 'I Have a Dream' speech
Profumo Affair

1964   Nelson Mandela sentenced to life imprisonment
Commercial pirate radio challenges BBC monopoly

1965   State funeral of Winston Churchill
US sends troops to Vietnam
A. L. Kennedy born in Dundee, Scotland

1966   Ian Brady and Myra Hindley sentenced to life
imprisonment for Moors Murders
England beats West Germany 4–2 at Wembley to win
Football World Cup
Star Trek series debut on NBC television
Jean Rhys, *The Wide Sargasso Sea*

1967   Six-Day War in the Middle East
World's first heart transplant
Abortion Act legalizes termination of pregnancy
in the UK
Sergeant Pepper's Lonely Hearts Club Band album released
by The Beatles
Flann O'Brien, *The Third Policeman*

1968   Anti-Vietnam War protestors attempt to storm
the American Embassy in Grosvenor Square
Martin Luther King Jr assassinated
Robert F. Kennedy assassinated
Student protests and riots in France
Lord Chamberlain's role as censor of plays in the UK
is abolished
Lindsay Anderson, *If . . .*

1969   Civil rights march in Northern Ireland attacked by
Protestants
Apollo 11 lands on the Moon with Neil Armstrong's
famous first steps
Rock concert at Woodstock

Yasser Arafat becomes leader of PLO
Booker Prize first awarded; winner P. H. Newby, *Something to Answer for*
Open University founded in the UK
John Fowles, *The French Lieutenant's Woman*

1970   Popular Front for the Liberation of Palestine (PFLP) hijacks five planes
Students activists and bystanders shot in anti–Vietnam War protest at Kent State University, Ohio; four killed, nine wounded
UK voting age reduced from 21 years to 18

1971   Decimal currency introduced in the UK
Internment without trial of terrorist suspects in Northern Ireland begins
India and Pakistan in conflict after Bangladesh declares independence

1972   Miners' Strike
Bloody Sunday in Londonderry, 14 protestors killed outright or fatally wounded by British troops
Aldershot barracks bomb initiates IRA campaign with seven dead
Britain enters the Common Market
Massacre of Israeli athletes at Munich Olympics
Watergate scandal
Anthony Burgess, *A Clockwork Orange*
Samuel Beckett, *Not I*

1973   US troops leave Vietnam
Arab–Israeli 15-day Yom Kippur War
PM Edward Heath introduces three-day working week
Martin Amis, *The Rachel Papers*

1974   Miners' Strike
IRA bombings in Guildford (5 dead) and Birmingham (21 dead)

1975   Microsoft founded
Sex Discrimination Act
Zadie Smith born in North London
Malcolm Bradbury, *The History Man*

1976   Weak economy forces UK government loan from the
International Monetary Fund (IMF)
Ian McEwan, *First Love, Last Rites*

1977   *Star Wars* released
UK unemployment tops 1,600,000
Nintendo begins to sell computer games
Sex Pistols 'Anarchy In the UK' tour

1978   Soviet troops occupy Afghanistan
First test-tube baby born in Oldham, England

1979   Iranian Revolution establishes Islamic theocracy
Margaret Thatcher becomes PM after Conservative
election victory
USSR invades Afghanistan
Lord Mountbatten assassinated by the IRA

1980   Iran–Iraq War starts
Iranian Embassy siege in London
CND rally at Greenham Common airbase, England
IRA hunger strike at Belfast Maze Prison over political
status for prisoners
Julian Barnes, *Metroland*

1981   Prince Charles and Lady Diana marry in St Paul's
Cathedral with 750 million worldwide television audience
Widespread urban riots in the UK including in Brixton,
Holloway, Toxteth,
Handsworth, Moss Side
AIDS identified

First IBM personal computer
Alasdair Gray, *Lanark*
Salman Rushdie, *Midnight's Children*, which wins Booker
Prize for Fiction

1982 Mark Thatcher, PM's son, disappears for three days in
Sahara during the Paris–Dakar rally
Falklands War with Argentina, costing the UK over
£1.6 billion
Body of Roberto Calvi, chairman of Vatican-connected
Banco Ambrosiano, found hanging beneath Blackfriars
Bridge, London

1983 Klaus Barbie, Nazi war criminal, arrested in Bolivia
Beirut: US Embassy and barracks bombing, killing
hundreds of members of multinational peacekeeping
force, mostly US marines
US troops invade Grenada
Microsoft Word first released
Salman Rushdie, *Shame* , which wins Prix du Meilleur
Livre Etranger (France)

1984 Miners' Strike
HIV identified as cause of AIDS
IRA bomb at Conservative Party Conference in Brighton
kills four British Telecom privatization shares sale
Thirty-eight deaths during clashes at Liverpool *v.*
Juventus football match at Heysel Stadium, Brussels
Martin Amis, *Money: A Suicide Note*
Julian Barnes, *Flaubert's Parrot*
James Kelman, *Busconductor Hines*
Graham Swift, *Waterland*

1985 Famine in Ethiopia and Live Aid concert
Damage to ozone layer discovered
Mikhail Gorbachev becomes Soviet Premier and
introduces *glasnost* (openness with the West) and
perestroika (economic restructuring)

PC Blakelock murdered during riots on Broadwater Farm
estate in Tottenham, London
My Beautiful Laundrette film released (dir. Stephen Frears,
screenplay Hanif Kureishi)
Jeanette Winterson, *Oranges Are Not the Only Fruit*

1986   Abolition of Greater London Council and other
metropolitan county councils in England
Violence between police and protestors at Wapping, East
London, after Rupert Murdoch sacks 5000 print workers
Challenger shuttle explodes
Chernobyl nuclear accident
US bombs Libya
Peter Ackroyd, *Hawksmoor*

1987   Capsizing of RORO ferry, *Herald of Free Enterprise*, off
Zeebrugge kills 193 people
London Stock Exchange and market collapse on
'Black Monday'
Remembrance Sunday: eleven killed by Provisional IRA
bomb in Enniskillen
Ian McEwan, *The Child in Time*, which wins Whitbread
Novel Award
Jeanette Winterson, *The Passion*

1988   US shoots down Iranian passenger flight
Pan Am flight 103 bombed over Lockerbie, 270 people
killed
Soviet troop withdrawals from Afghanistan begin
Salman Rushdie, *The Satanic Verses*

1989   Fatwa issued against Rushdie by Iranian leadership
(Khomeini)
The Fall of the Berlin Wall
Exxon Valdez oil disaster
Student protestors massacred in Tiananmen Square,
Beijing

Hillsborough Stadium disaster in which 96 football
fans die
Kazuo Ishiguro, *The Remains of the Day*, which wins
Booker Prize for Fiction
Jeanette Winterson, *Sexing the Cherry*

1990   London poll tax riots
Fall of Thatcher; John Major becomes Conservative PM
Nelson Mandela freed from jail
Jeanette Winterson adapts *Oranges* for BBC television film
A. S. Byatt, *Possession*
Hanif Kureishi, *The Buddha of Suburbia*, which wins
Whitbread Best First Novel Prize
A. L. Kennedy, *Night Geometry and the Garscadden Trains*

1991   Soviet Union collapses
First Iraq War with 12-day Operation Desert Storm
Apartheid ended in South Africa
PM Major negotiates opt-out for Britain from European
Monetary Union and rejects Social Chapter of the
Maastricht Treaty
Hypertext Markup Language (HTML) helps create the
World Wide Web
Hanif Kureishi: screenplays for *Sammy and Rosie Get Laid*
and *London Kills Me*
Pat Barker, *Regeneration*

1992   'Black Wednesday' stock market crisis when UK forced
to exit European Exchange Rate Mechanism
Adam Thorpe, *Ulverton*
Jeanette Winterson, *Written on the Body*

1993   Black teenager Stephen Lawrence murdered in Well Hall
Road, London
With Downing Street Declaration, PM John Major and
Taoiseach Albert Reynolds commit Britain and Ireland to
joint Northern Ireland resolution

Film of Ishiguro's *The Remains of the Day*, starring
Anthony Hopkins and Emma Thompson
Irvine Welsh, *Trainspotting*

1994   Tony Blair elected leader of Labour Party following death
of John Smith
Channel Tunnel opens
Nelson Mandela elected President of South Africa
Provisional IRA and loyalist paramilitary ceasefire
Homosexual age of consent for men in the UK
lowered to 18
Mike Newell (dir.), *Four Weddings and a Funeral*
Jonathan Coe, *What a Carve Up!*
James Kelman, *How late it was, how late*, which wins Booker
Prize for Fiction
Irvine Welsh, *The Acid House*
Jeanette Winterson, *Art & Lies: A Piece for Three Voices
and a Bawd*

1995   Oklahoma City bombing
Srebrenica massacre during Bosnian War
Pat Barker, *The Ghost Road*
Nicholas Hytner (dir.), *The Madness of King George*
Hanif Kureishi, *The Black Album*

1996   Cases of Bovine Spongeiform Encephalitis (Mad Cow
Disease) in the UK
Divorce of Charles and Diana
Breaching ceasefire, Provisional IRA bombs London's
Canary Wharf and Central Manchester
Film of Irvine Welsh's *Trainspotting* (dir. Danny Boyle),
starring Ewan McGregor and Robert Carlyle
Graham Swift, *Last Orders*, which wins Booker Prize

1997   Tony Blair becomes Labour PM after landslide victory
Princess Diana dies in Paris car crash
Hong Kong returned to China by the UK

Jim Crace, *Quarantine*
Jonathan Coe, *The House of Sleep*, which wins Prix Médicis
Etranger (France)
Ian McEwan, *Enduring Love*
Iain Sinclair and Marc Atkins, *Lights Out for the Territory*
Jeanette Winterson, *Gut Symmetries*

1998   Good Friday Agreement on Northern Ireland and
Northern Ireland Assembly established
Twenty-eight people killed by splinter group Real IRA
bombing in Omagh
Sonny Bono Act extends copyright to lifetime plus
70 years
BFI/Channel 4 film *Stella Does Tricks* released (screenplay
A. L. Kennedy)
Julian Barnes, *England, England*

1999   Euro currency adopted
Macpherson Inquiry into Stephen Lawrence murder
accuses London's Metropolitan Police of institutional
racism
NATO bombs Serbia over Kosovo crisis
Welsh Assembly and Scottish Parliament both open
Thirty-one passengers killed in Ladbroke Grove train
disaster

2000   Anti-globalization protest and riots in London
Hauliers and farmers blockade oil refineries in fuel price
protest in the UK
Kazuo Ishiguro, *When We Were Orphans*
Will Self, *How the Dead Live*
Zadie Smith, *White Teeth*
Jeanette Winterson, *The PowerBook*

2001   9/11 Al-Qaeda attacks on World Trade Center and
Pentagon
Bombing and invasion of Afghanistan

Riots in Oldham, Leeds, Bradford and Burnley,
Northern England
Labour Party under Blair re-elected to government
Ian McEwan, *Atonement*

2002   Queen Mother dies aged 101
Rowan Williams named next Archbishop of Canterbury
Bali terrorist bomb kills 202 people and injures a
further 209
Inquiry concludes English general practitioner Dr Harold
Shipman killed around 215 patients
Zadie Smith's *White Teeth* adapted for Channel 4 television
broadcast in autumn

2003   Invasion of Iraq and fall of Saddam Hussein
Death of UK government scientist Dr David Kelly, and
Hutton Inquiry
Worldwide threat of Severe Acute Respiratory Syndrome
(SARS)

2004   BBC Director General Greg Dyke steps down over
Kelly affair
Bombings in Madrid kill 190 people and injure over 1700
Expansion of NATO to include seven ex–Warsaw Pact
countries
European Union expands to 25 countries as eight
ex-communist states join
Jonathan Coe, *Like a Fiery Elephant: The Story of B. S. Johnson*
Alan Hollinghurst, *The Line of Beauty*, which wins Booker
Prize for Fiction
Andrea Levy, *Small Island*, which wins Orange Prize for
Fiction
Jeanette Winterson, *Lighthousekeeping*

2005   UK ban on fox-hunting with dogs comes into force
7/7 London suicide bombings on transport system kill
52 and injure over 700 commuters in morning rush hour

Hurricane Katrina kills at least 1836 people and floods
devastate New Orleans
After four failed bombings are detected, Brazilian Jean
Charles de Menezes is shot and killed by Metropolitan
Police officers at Stockwell Underground Station
Ian McEwan, *Saturday*
Zadie Smith, *On Beauty*, which wins 2006 Orange Prize
for Fiction
Jeanette Winterson, *Weight*

2006   Jeanette Winterson awarded the OBE
Airline terror plot thwarted, causes major UK airline
delays
Israel–Hezbollah war in Lebanon
Five prostitutes killed in Ipswich in a six-week period
Saddam Hussein executed by hanging in controversial
circumstances
Jeanette Winterson, *Tanglewreck*

1

INTRODUCTION

> I keep telling this story – different people, different places,
> different times – but always you, always me, always this
> story, because a story is a tightrope between two worlds.
>
> (*The PowerBook*, p. 119)

Since the mid-1980s and the publication of her debut novel,
Oranges Are Not the Only Fruit, Jeanette Winterson has established herself as a significant figure in the field of contemporary
British literature and as a popular writer for study in schools
and universities.[1] In a country not given to lauding its writers, Winterson occupies an interesting and significant role in the
nation's contemporary cultural life. Sales for her particular style
of literary fiction have been consistently good, and she is regularly invited to judge prizes and give her opinions on television
programmes about arts and culture.[2] Winterson's recognition by
the cultural establishment is epitomized by the award of an OBE
bestowed on her in 2006.

This book aims to provide a timely, critically informed
overview of the full range of Jeanette Winterson's works, locating
them in the contexts of contemporary culture and literary history. In addition to offering a comprehensive critical survey of her
texts, the study will discuss the many controversial aspects of the
Winterson *oeuvre* and persona, seeking to account for her mixed
critical response. The study will also address seeming contradictions in Winterson's work such as its thoroughly postmodern
stylistics on the one hand and its commitment to transcendent

notions of love, art and the imagination on the other. In addition, it will examine the way in which her work pushes simultaneously in two directions, towards a universalist address to a general readership and towards a more specific treatment of lesbian and feminist concerns.

This introduction considers the various constructions of Winterson the writer, placing her work in a number of key contexts. First, I discuss Winterson's writing in relation to the British novel since the 1980s, looking at its status as literary fiction. I turn to a consideration of the particular paradigms upon which her work draws, including anti-realist, postmodernist and feminist traditions, all of which provide a context for reading the multiple border crossings and fantastic journeys through space, time, genre and gender undertaken in her texts. My study of Winterson starts with a consideration of the author's life in relation to her work and concludes with a discussion of her writing beyond the novel form and her most recent work.

WINTERSON AS A CONTEMPORARY BRITISH WRITER

Winterson's writing career began in the mid-1980s, at the same time as a generation of British writers including Martin Amis, Angela Carter, Ian McEwan, Salman Rushdie and Julian Barnes, all of them publishing major works. *Oranges Are Not the Only Fruit* came out a year after Carter's *Nights at the Circus* and Amis's *Money: A Suicide Note*, and four years after Rushdie's *Midnight's Children*. Such writers had written their apprentice works during the 1970s; Winterson's experience was different in that her first novel brought her to sudden prominence. Her immediate contemporaries include Graham Swift, who published *Waterland* in 1984; Peter Ackroyd, whose *Hawksmoor* came out in 1986; and Kazuo Ishiguro, whose *Remains of the Day* was published in 1989. This mid–late 1980s generation was followed by another which included Hanif Kureishi and A. L. Kennedy, their first work published in 1990.

If one considers the historical timeline included at the beginning of this book, it is apparent that the 1980s, when Winterson and her fellow writers established themselves, were a period of intense social and political upheaval. The decade began and ended with riots in major British cities (over racism and social exclusion in 1981 and the infamous poll tax in 1990). The early 1980s saw the consolidation of Thatcherism, a combination of monetarist policies, military aggression and hostility to unionized labour, which resulted in the Falklands War of 1982 and the Miners' Strike of 1984–1985. Despite the imperial bravado, the outcome was mass unemployment and the further decline of manufacturing and heavy industry. Moreover, throughout the decade the British state was under attack from a series of lethal IRA bombing campaigns. The late 1980s saw the Stock Exchange collapse on 'Black Monday' and 'negative equity' in the housing market; Thatcher's own downfall followed in 1990 when she was voted out of office by her own Party. International politics were no less eventful: the decade began with the Iran–Iraq war and ended just before the 1991 US invasion of Iraq. A series of human and environmental disasters included famine in Ethiopia (1985) and the nuclear accident at Chernobyl (1986). In the Communist bloc the Berlin Wall fell in 1989, two years before the collapse of the Soviet Union.

What is noticeable about the literature produced by British writers during this period is how infrequently it responds directly to the contemporary moment. It tends not to be overtly political and 'social realism' is virtually absent.[3] Amis is unusual in tackling head-on the sexy, greedy 1980s in his 1984 satire, *Money*, albeit in an anti-realist satiric form. Indeed, Winterson noted that

> I wrote *The Passion* in 1986, boom-time of the Thatcher years, clock-race of yuppies and City boys, rich-quick, never count the cost. My own cities were invented; cities of language, cities of connection, worlds as gangways and bridges to the cities of the interior where the coin was not money, where it was all emotion.
>
> (Note to 1996 Vintage edition)

In her 2000 review of *The PowerBook*, Elaine Showalter (2000) criticizes the smallness of vision of many contemporary British writers including Winterson. She laments the fact that in the highly political years leading up to the millennium, Winterson's work still seemed preoccupied with romantic triangles and 'the journeys of the mind' rather than treating social themes and the 'big Balzacian questions of the day' (*ibid.*). But critics who say that

Winterson eschews politics are incorrect, misreading her privileging of the aesthetic realm and her anti-realism as hostility to 'real' issues. Indeed, as Peter Childs has argued, *The Passion* is 'a book in which Winterson created an imaginative "mirror" to the actual world of the Thatcher boom years ... not a looking glass but a reflector of possibilities' (2005, p.256). And, while Winterson rejects the label 'political' writer – as she rejects labels of all kinds – her work is suffused with a sense of political injustice and protest. It is combative, impassioned, speaking up on behalf of history's silent majorities and minorities – women, gay people and the working class – on a range of subjects including capitalism, patriarchy, and war. In this respect it could be argued that Winterson's work contributes towards the creation of what the cultural theorist Michel Foucault has termed 'counter memory', which works against the grain of orthodox history to acknowledge alternative 'subjugated knowledges' (Marshall, 1992).

Frequently, contemporary British writers have turned to *style*, adopting postmodern aesthetic techniques of parody, pastiche and metafiction, in order to maintain an ironic distance from the contemporary. Repeatedly in literary fiction of the period there is an obsessive interest in the writing of history (*Midnight's Children*, *Nights at the Circus*, *Waterland*, *Hawksmoor*, *Sexing the Cherry*); a preoccupation with identity and selfhood as a fictional construction (*Money*, *Oranges*); and a sustained questioning of the limitations of realist aesthetics (as in all of the above). In this respect Winterson is typical of this generation of contemporary British writers: the absence of a referential frame is particularly apparent in Winterson's works of the 1980s and 1990s, which eschew realism for an exploration of language in a series of invented pasts and fantasy worlds.

WINTERSON AS A (POST)MODERNIST WRITER

Winterson is indisputably a writer in the tradition of modernist and postmodernist metafiction. But whether she should be more properly described as a modernist or a postmodernist is open to debate. While it is clear that Winterson would like to be known as a modernist 'in the European tradition of Borges and Calvino' (2002, p. 2), most academic commentators to date have discussed her work in the context of postmodernism. For example, as early as 1992 Patricia Waugh included her as a critical postmodernist alongside Angela Carter; more recently, the essays in *Jeanette Winterson: A Contemporary Critical Guide* designated her as a key postmodern stylist. As Grice and Woods observe,

> Jeanette Winterson's prominence as a contemporary British writer who self-consciously explores the equivocal status of an objective reality is largely due to her persistent metafictional interrogation of the assumptions about narratorial identity, fictional artifice and objective reality.
>
> (2007, p. 29)

Critics have recently begun to take seriously Winterson's claims to modernism. Susana Onega's 2006 study, for example, places Winterson in 'an international experimentalist trend' (p. 2) and discusses the influences of modernist writers such as Eliot and Woolf on her work.

How useful is it to distinguish between these modes in relation to Winterson's work? Literary critics and academics like to differentiate between modernist and postmodernist periods, literary techniques and strategies, but writers are not as interested in formal boundaries and demarcations, and may well draw on numerous past traditions as Eliot advocates in his seminal essay of poetic modernism, 'Tradition and the individual talent' (1932). Winterson is clearly a modernist in the sense that not only is she an experimenter with fictional forms, but she views art as an ultimate value (as did Woolf, Eliot and Joyce). Indeed, in *Art Objects* she retains the distinction between 'real' art and popular culture, arguing that only art is capable of challenging our sense of ourselves and remaking the language (p. 15).

For her part, Winterson seems resistant to postmodernism, perhaps in common with many writers – and increasingly with academic critics – believing it to be a faddish phenomenon compared to the gravitas of the modernist canon. She complains in *Art Objects* that in the late twentieth century we are 'entirely fenced in with posts' (p. 6). Above all, Winterson associates postmodernism with the mass media, towards which she is ambivalent, and with a loss of authorial control and aesthetic value, both of which are of course prized by modernism. 'You are a slave to advertising, to fashion, to habit and to the media', she charges the reader in

Art & Lies (p. 186). The way out of such slavery, for Winterson, is to return to real ideas which are to be found in books.

As in modernism, Winterson insists on the discreteness and integrity of the artistic realm. The epigraph to her most experimental novel, *Art & Lies*, included a quote from Bradley's 1901 'Oxford Lectures on Poetry', which articulates an exemplary rejection of art as *mimesis* or imitation:

> The nature of a work of art is to be not a part, nor yet a copy of the real world (as we commonly understand that phrase), but a world in itself, independent, complete, autonomous; and to possess it fully you must enter that world, conform to its laws, and ignore for the time the beliefs, aims, and particular conditions which belong to you in the other world of reality.
>
> (*AL*, epigraph)

She places herself in the tradition of Virginia Woolf, Gertrude Stein and T.S. Eliot as a committed experimenter with literary form and genre. As Lucasta Miller avers, 'Winterson has a strong sense of literary tradition combined with an impulse towards innovation' (Miller, 2005). In an echo of Ezra Pound's phrase 'make it new', Winterson believes that the writer's vocation above all is to remake language, stating in *Written*, 'it's the clichés that cause the trouble' (p. 71). Like Eliot, Winterson distances art from the writer's 'experience' in favour of the created, crafted 'emotion'. This desire to experiment with language can be seen to a greater or lesser extent in all Winterson's work: from the fantastic and metafictional interludes of texts like *Oranges* and *PowerBook* to the more radical deformation of language and literary form carried out in *Art & Lies*, her aim has been 'to test experience against language and language against experience' (*AO*, p. 79). In *Art & Lies*, Winterson expresses a fear that language is moribund – 'Delicate words exhausted through overuse' (p. 65) – and her work attests to her attempts to resuscitate language.

While Winterson has stated that she does not think of herself as a poet, nevertheless her work does strive towards the condition of poetry. As she states, 'I think of myself as somebody who tries to use poetic disciplines and align them in a narrative stretch' (Reynolds and Noakes, 2003, p. 22). In other words, she tries to imbue her language with a poetic density in which 'every word should do its work' (*ibid.*). Since *Written on the Body* Winterson has adopted a literary style, traceable back to Anglo-Saxon poetry through to the poetry of Ted Hughes, which makes much use of alliterative compound nouns and blunt Saxon terminology as in the following description of Scott's dogs in *Lighthousekeeping*:

> Not earth-bound anymore, he could wing the dogs in a wind-ruff of fur, husky-haloed through two miles or so of gravity, then out, free, barking at the moon, half-wolf, half-tame, going home to the white planet he had seen shining in their orange eyes, paws hock-deep in snow.

> (*L*, p. 63)

In her essay collection, *Art Objects*, which serves as her aesthetic manifesto, Winterson defends the otherness of art, stating 'All art is a foreign city' (p. 4). Like the modernists whose ideas she champions, Winterson also believes that art should be difficult and challenging, arguing that 'true art . . . challenges the "I" that we are' (p. 15). The key theme of these essays is that art is both central to human life and eternal. They endorse what Onega calls her 'mythopoeic and transcendentalist vision of art' (2006, p. 9). Winterson adopts a quasi-religious attitude towards art as 'living spirit' suggesting that it replaces the evangelical religion of her youth. Indeed, her work may be seen as representing an extended 'hymn to the book' (*AL*, p. 202).

We must as critics take seriously Winterson as a modernist writer, not least because this is how she views her own work. However, she is also indubitably a postmodernist engaged in a playful and parodic rescripting of popular and canonical genres, and in the construction of reality as precisely an intricate web of fictional worlds, of endless stories. Winterson's novels clearly exemplify a postmodern aesthetics, demonstrating high levels of temporal dislocation, self-reflexivity, intertextuality and pastiche. Gavin Keulks identifies her dominant themes and tropes – 'existential contingency and spectacle, the performative nature of gender and identity, the ontological burdens of love' – as 'quintessentially postmodern' (2007, p. 147). Moreover, her work participates in the subversion of the liberal humanist grand narratives of Knowledge, Truth, Meaning and History (Lyotard, 1984). In fiction and non-fiction works Winterson has challenged the tenets of classical realism to the extent that, as Onega comments, 'her suspicion of realism is such that she even disparages one of her own most valuable and distinctive features: storytelling' (2006, p. 10). According to Keulks, 'over the course of ten novels she has evolved a signature blend of postmodern prose, a mélange of Linda Hutcheon's "historiographic metafiction", Diane Elam's "postmodern romance", and Amy J. Elias's "metahistorical romance"' (2007, p. 147). In an exemplary fashion, Winterson's work performs the ironic reworking of history characteristic of 'historiographic metafiction', which, according to Hutcheon, claims 'that its world is both resolutely fictive and yet undeniably historical, and that what both realms share is their constitution in and as discourse' (1989, p. 142). In *The Passion* and *Sexing the Cherry*, history is recast as story to be retold and reinvented in ways that foreground its arbitrariness and constructedness. The political and critical element identified by Hutcheon is present in the voices of the 'little people' Winterson seeks to capture, and in the marginalia and minutiae of life and love that she writes in the gaps of the larger, canonical stories – the Civil War and Napoleon's invasion of Russia. In *The Passion* Henri distrusts stories despite or perhaps because of his repeated assurance 'I'm telling you stories, trust me' (p. 13). As Winterson opines, 'People have an enormous need to separate history, which is fact, from storytelling, which is not fact . . . and the whole push of my work has been to say, you cannot know which is which' (Harthill, 1990).

To argue that the distinguishing feature of *post*modernism resides in the absence of any metanarrative and a thoroughgoing cultural relativism is to imply that a whole generation of British writers including Winterson is not in fact postmodernist. While Winterson and her fellow experimentalists such as Carter, Amis and Barnes deconstruct the categories of identity, history, meaning, truth, they do not abjure value altogether. Monika Mueller argues that Winterson's relation to postmodernism is a 'contested category' (2001, p. 42) and Keulks argues persuasively that her work represents a crossroads or 'a bifurcation within postmodernism itself', one which rescues the categories of history and love from 'postmodern exhaustion' (2007, p. 147). A simplistic modernist/postmodernist distinction would also exclude the work of a group of writers who share a postmodern stylistics with a concern for social and political issues. Stylistically drawn towards postmodernism, politically and morally, Winterson, like Angela Carter, is deeply critical of it. In addition to her strong anti-patriarchal and feminist message, all her work includes a critique of aspects of contemporary capitalism and the popular culture it has given rise to, in particular the loss of values other than the monetary. Despite her commitment to a postmodern aesthetics of fragmentation, metafiction, intertextuality, parody and hybridity, and to certain postmodern epistemological tenets such as fluidity and instability of self and world and the ultimate unknowability of things, Winterson contests the postmodern abandonment of metanarratives and the idea that there is no intrinsic value.

Winterson's work in a fantasy mode may therefore be seen as an indirect response to the oppressiveness of social and political reality. As Rosemary Jackson identified, fantasy represents 'a literature of subversion', *by other means* (my emphasis) (1981). Just as in the magic realism of Borges, Márquez and Grass, fantasy offers readers an alternative to repressive regimes and material constraints – particularly of gender, sexuality and class in Winterson's case. Another postmodern concept, 'virtual corporeality' (Sofia, 1999), an oxymoron suggesting an impossible combination, is also extremely useful in thinking about Winterson's relation to the real and her engagement with the contemporary moment. Winterson's texts are peopled with similar impossible combinations: gender and species hybrids such as the Dog Woman in *Sexing the Cherry*, the web-footed Villanelle in *The Passion*, and trans-sexual time-travellers like Ali/Alix in *The PowerBook*. By blending the real and the imagined in such 'cyborg' fusions, Winterson's work simultaneously offers a critique of the status quo and gestures towards utopian possibilities beyond it.

WINTERSON AS A LESBIAN/FEMINIST WRITER

"When is a text a 'lesbian text' or its writer a 'lesbian writer'?" Bonnie Zimmerman posed this question in 1981 and it is one that has concerned critics and students of Winterson's work since the publication of *Oranges* a few years later. Zimmerman warns against a narrowly sexual definition of lesbianism, adding that it 'leads to the identification of literature with life, which can be an overly defensive and suspect strategy' (1986, p. 221). This is an issue of particular relevance to Winterson, a contemporary writer whose sexual orientation is well known and who came out early in her career. While Winterson acknowledges the importance of lesbian desire in her work, she rejects the term 'lesbian writer' (see Chapter 6).[4] Of course the term carries an ambiguity, depending on whether the prefix is used as an adjective or as part of the noun. Winterson would rather be known as a *'writer* who loves women' than as a lesbian *who writes* (my emphasis) and she insists on a separation between art and life: 'I know that the language of my passion and the language of my art are not the same thing' (*AO*, p. 105). Thus, she is not a writer whose lesbianism defines her work or whose work is 'by, for and about' lesbians, in the sense that the discipline of Women's Studies is 'by, for and about' women. In this regard, Winterson is not repudiating lesbianism *per se*, merely lesbian identity as a restricting identity category. She therefore adopts Judith Butler's (2004) theory that identity categories operate as 'regulatory regimes', and follows the practice of many women writers who reject the label 'woman' or 'feminist' writer for similar reasons. One such is Margaret Atwood, whose work has a close and rich relationship to second wave feminism, but who rejects the term 'feminist writer' as restricting. Feminists, or lesbians for that matter, do not need to feel let down or betrayed (see Pearce, 1998) by this positioning on the part of (women) writers. It is an inevitable, and surely admirable, ambition of writers to wish to speak to readers as a whole and for their work to have a 'universal' reach.

In a follow-up essay in 1992, Zimmerman argued that the term 'lesbian' in theoretical discourse has been 'positioned as a metaphor for the radical disruption of dominant systems and discourses' (1992, p. 12). Her observation is useful in analysing the ways in which Winterson writes about lesbianism. Rather than holding a mirror up to nature, or writing about real lesbian lives, Winterson is using aspects of experience to make new literary and sexual meanings. Moreover, much of Winterson's writing corresponds to the tendency of lesbian fiction, outlined by Terry Castle (1990), to oscillate between the realistic and the fabulous. Given that the mimetic literary mode has traditionally silenced female homosociality, argues Castle, lesbian writing continually pushes out of mimeticism into the fantastic and fabulous modes, opening up into the terrain of the implausible. Virginia Woolf's *Orlando*, which Winterson has acknowledged as a key influence on her work, is a celebrated example of this strategy. Ostensibly based on the 'life' of Woolf's lover Vita Sackville-West, the novel combines a history of literary forms, a philosophical meditation on the meaning of historical time, an analysis of the relationship between sex and gender and a fantasy narrative of the experience of an immortal, cross-dressing figure as he/she moves through the centuries. The fantasy premise of the novel allows for the representation of a lesbian subject ultimately unconstrained by the social conventions of gender.

Sharing the deconstructive emphasis of Winterson's writing, the discourse of queer theory sets out to challenge heterosexist master narratives, not least the binary opposition between heterosexuality and homosexuality that renders the latter marginal and illegitimate. As Childs observes, 'Much of Winterson's writing aims at taking apart binaries . . . and replacing them with symmetries' (2005, p. 263). In respect of the representation of gender and sexuality, Winterson's work seems to epitomize what Eve Sedgwick, a key figure in the development of queer theory, has called 'open mesh of possibilities, gaps, overlaps, dissonances and resonances, lapses and excesses of meaning when the constituent elements of anyone's gender, of anyone's sexuality aren't made (or can't be made) to signify monolithically' (1994, p. 8). However, while Winterson's work features numerous queer devices such as proliferating sexual identities, presenting gender as masquerade and denaturalizing heterosexuality, Winterson has professed herself resistant to what she sees as the reductive nature of Queer culture more generally. She states, 'The Queer world has colluded in the misreading of art as sexuality. Art is difference, but not necessarily sexual difference, and while to be outside of the mainstream of imposed choice is likely to make someone more conscious, it does not necessarily make them an artist' (AO, p. 104).

My work has consistently addressed Winterson's relationship to a lesbian aesthetic tradition (2005, 2006, 2007), while also recognizing her ambivalence towards the concept. In this study I contend that Winterson seeks to write about desire *per se* and that this depiction is frequently grounded in lesbian experience, using that experience as a take-off point, continually reaching beyond particular bodies, selves and actions for the universal. While an ideological reading of her work can certainly – indeed must inevitably – be made, it is not reducible to sexual politics, any more than the work of Atwood, Carter, Amis or McEwan. To borrow Rachel Blau du Plessis's (1990) phrase, Winterson is a 'both/and' writer, not an 'either/or' writer, continually signifying gendered meanings and continually calling them into question.

If Winterson frequently distances herself and her work from essentialist expressions of 'lesbian culture', and from the sexualizing tendencies of a queer lens, it is relatively easy to trace the feminist aspects of her writing. In particular, her work resonates both stylistically and thematically with what Hélène Cixous (1981) calls écriture féminine, a simultaneously poetical and political writing that represents the feminine as both an alternative to and a critique of the masculine or phallocentric symbolic order. Cixous views feminine writing as an extension of the female body – 'Text: my body – shot through with streams of song' (1981, p. 253), characterizing both as heterogeneous: 'you can't talk about a female sexuality, uniform, homogeneous, classifiable into codes . . . Women's imaginary is inexhaustible' (p. 246). As in much of Winterson's work, écriture féminine posits a connection between (women's) bodies, voices and texts, and represent the text itself as a kind of sexed body.

From *Oranges* on, her work is consistently critical of heterosexual and male privilege and ferociously anti-marriage; almost every novel contains a critique of, if not a diatribe against, the institution which she sees as stifling and domesticating love and giving a specious state and church imprimatur to human relationships. Of *Oranges* Winterson states, 'It exposes the sanctity of family life as something of a sham; it illustrates by example that what the church calls love is actually a psychosis and it dares to suggest that what makes life difficult for homosexuals is not their perversity but other people's' (O, p. xiii). A decade later on, in *Art & Lies*, Winterson questions women's supposed heterosexual orientation and the basis for it: 'She had been told that many women looked at a man and wanted his children. She could understand that but marriage became survival and economics' (p. 82). Furthermore, she challenges the view of right-wing Christian thinkers such as Roger Scruton that married love is both natural and God-given, putting the feminist argument that it is historically, socially and materially constituted. Winterson presents marriage as a conveyor-belt approach to human relationships, and a lemming-like act of conformity: 'Down the aisle they went, for better for worse, for richer for poorer, in sickness and in health', 'till Death do us part. Death did part them; dead to feeling, dead to beauty, dead to all but the most obvious pleasures . . . ' (*AL*, p. 83).

Just as feminist literature in the 1970s confronted patriarchal myths and stereotypes about women, so from the mid-1980s writers like Winterson began to deconstruct the myths of feminist discourse. In common with third wave and postmodern feminists, Winterson resists the victim motif that sometimes characterized radical and cultural feminist discourse in the 1970s and 1980s. Like Angela Carter, Winterson is a 'demythologizer' or debunker of myths of gender, whatever their source. Her use of the anti-romance mode represents an ideological choice, a refusal of traditional 'naturally female' imagery and a bold reclamation of words from patriarchal usage. Like Angela Carter, she appropriates 'male' pornographic language and resituates it, frequently to empower women as in the highly experimental *Art & Lies*.

MAJOR THEMES IN WINTERSON'S WORK

I identify three overarching themes, which may be termed 'metanarratives', informing Winterson's entire oeuvre. First, she presents love as a transcendent value, independent of social institutions such as marriage and the family (as I discussed above, a strong anti-marriage critique is present in all her works). Secondly, she presents art as an absolute value through time, and as a corollary, storytelling as a constant means of expression in human life (*GS*, p. 153–154). Thirdly, and apparently paradoxically, Winterson represents 'reality' and 'identity' as radically unstable concepts, whereby the 'self' and the world it inhabits are continually in flux.

The abiding theme of Winterson's work is love: yearning and unfulfilled desire, the risks of falling in love with another person, sexual passion and breaking up are universal themes that all her novels explore in various ways. As Susana Onega states, love represents 'the central single vision around which all her fictions develop' (2006, p. 8). Winterson's novels may be seen as a kind of prose poem celebrating the power of love; in *Gut Symmetries* she states, 'Love bears all things, believes all things, hopes all things, endures all things. Love never ends' (p. 164). And in *Written*, Winterson anatomizes love to explore the question posed on the opening page: 'Why is the measure of love loss?' (p. 9). In these texts and throughout her work, Winterson seeks a means of expressing love in a way that both draws on and goes beyond the conventions of the romance tradition. As Childs observes, 'To love differently emerges as a goal achieved by telling stories differently, of re-imagining and re-mapping life' (2005, p. 261). She wants to find a truly universal mode of expression that speaks to all lovers regardless of gender and sexuality. 'I love you', the Jekyll and Hyde figure, Babel Dark, says in *Lighthousekeeping*: 'The three most difficult words in the world' (p. 100). Winterson frequently pits romantic passion against the demands and compromises of domestic life. And although she often parodies romantic excess, her work is largely hostile to domesticity; as she states in *Written on the Body*, 'Love belongs to itself' (p. 77) and 'marriage is the flimsiest weapon against desire' (p. 78). Like the twelfth-century troubadours, who articulated the concept of courtly love, Winterson believes that marriage is inimical to true passion and only love freely given is worth the name. Perhaps, too, her work expresses the desire to cut loose, become a marriage renegade and have the freedom to love and leave.

One of the most common tropes in Winterson's work is the metaphor of lovemaking as writing. Repeatedly in her work the body is figured as a kind of text which the lover 'reads'. In *Art & Lies*, Sappho wears a 'sonnet on each breast' (p. 63) and entreats her lover to 'read me. Read me now' (p. 144). As a corollary to the metaphor of writing, Winterson's work consistently invokes this metaphor of reading. Ginette Carpenter argues that *Written on the Body*, *Art & Lies* and *The PowerBook* focus upon the body and desire in order to foreground the complexity of the reading process: 'Using the body and the enactment of bodily desire/s as a metaphor for the act of reading means that reading becomes, alongside love and art, something that can transform and . . . change lives' (2007, p. 79).

Winterson often places the theme of love in the context of a quest narrative, a mode that she sees as fundamental to storytelling. 'My search for you, your search for me, is a search after something that cannot be found' (*PB*, p. 78), she writes, implying that it is desire itself that impels narrative. All her novels contain questing heroes, sometimes female, sometimes male: Jeanette in *Oranges* begins the series; Henri and Jordan follow; more recently Silver appears in the adult novel *Lighthousekeeping* and the children's book *Tanglewreck*. In some texts, the hero is both sexes simultaneously: the nameless narrator in *Written* and the androgynous Ali/Alix in *The PowerBook*. All these questing figures are searching for love and for meaning, motivated by the idea that 'In this life you have to be your own hero' (*PB*, p. 155).

Winterson's work consistently attests to the power of storytelling in human life. In *Weight*, Winterson, adopting her authorial persona, writes, 'That's why I write fiction – so that I can keep telling the story' (p. 137). Apparently referring to her own childhood experience, she adds, 'My journeys [into books] were matters of survival; crossing nights of misery into days of hope. Keeping the light on was keeping the world going' (p. 139). The oft-repeated refrain of her novels runs, 'Trust me. I'm telling you stories' (*P*, p. 40). Elsewhere, in an interview with Louise Tucker, she foregrounds the idea of narrative as a kind of sense-making and cognitive mapping of the world:

> Storytelling is a way of establishing connections, imaginative connections for ourselves, a way of joining up disparate material and making sense of the world. Human beings love patterns; they love to see shapes and symmetries. We seem to have a need to impose order on our surroundings, which are generally chaotic and often themselves seem to lack any continuity, any storyline.
>
> (Winterson, 2005, p. 4)

Susana Onega (2006) picks up on a contradiction in Winterson's attitude to the novel: she disparages realism with its focus on narrative storytelling, yet extols storytelling as a human need and aesthetic principle. This reflects the postmodernist's ambivalence to storytelling: she wants to both tell stories and deconstruct them.

Winterson's work is highly intertextual, reworking fairy tales, Arthurian legend, works from the canon of Western literature and, in *Weight*, classical myth. As she commented in the introduction to the novella,

> My work is full of Cover Versions. I like to take stories we think
> we know and record them differently. In the re-telling comes a new
> emphasis or bias, and the new arrangement of the key elements
> demands that fresh material be injected into the existing text.
>
> (p. xviii)

These motifs are replayed throughout her work and reappear
through the repetition of key phrases or refrains. For example, the
phrases 'written on the body is a secret code', 'Trust me, I'm telling
you stories', 'we are empty space and points of light', 'to avoid discovery I stay on the run' and 'I want to tell the story again' recur
repeatedly in her novels, demonstrating Winterson's belief that
language is citational and carries with it the echo of past uses. This
corresponds to Bakhtin's (1981) view of language as dialogic, and
Barthes's (1977) view of writing as an 'intertextual' tissue of quota-
tions. Indeed, Winterson's work is thoroughly intertextual in the
sense that the different books are engaged in a dialogue with each
other. The same phrases recur, carrying with them the echo of past
usage and becoming re-signified in the new context. As Jennifer
Gustar comments,

> When Winterson writes that she wants to tell the story again, to
> which story does she refer? The story of Atlas and Heracles [in *Weight*],
> clearly, but is she also revisiting the story of *Written on the Body* which
> she cites and which is also itself a retelling of romance narratives
> lamenting the narrator's collusion in 'the same story every time'?
> This reiteration and self-reference suggest that perhaps Winterson is
> always cunningly engaged in her own literary critique.
>
> (2007, p. 58)

In this way Winterson evokes what Butler (1993, p. 225) calls
the 'citational legacy' of her own subjectivity in relation to her
own body of work. The significance of reading and re-reading
in Winterson's work is explored by Carpenter who highlights
'Winterson's own reading and re-presenting of canonical works'
in ways which work to 'blur the conventional distinctions between
author, reader and text. The author is also the re/reader; the reader
"writes" the work; the text is a site that shifts its significance, that
is continuously in flux' (2007, p. 70).

In contrast to her belief in art and love as transcendent values, Winterson rejects the idea of historical truth. Her work promotes ontological relativism and a subjective understanding of

the world, rejecting the idea of a fixed self and the belief in an objective, knowable reality 'out there'. The 2005 novella *Weight* appears to quote *Sexing the Cherry* of 1989 and to reaffirm this quintessentially postmodern aesthetic: 'Science is a story. History is a story...what am I? Atoms [...] Empty space and points of light' (p. 145, emphasis in original). The whole of *Art Objects* represents a restatement of the view that 'the only boundaries are the boundaries of the imagination' (p. 116). Winterson continually returns to the idea that the self is not fixed and that we live many lives simultaneously. 'What is identity?', she asks in *Art & Lies*, answering that it is 'the accumulation of parts', a series of objects, texts and events that construct 'myself' (p. 187). Her work draws on diverse discourses from fairy tale to Quantum Physics to convey her sense of the multifariousness of life and to give flesh to her belief that 'nothing is fixed'. 'I know that I am false', says Handel in *Art & Lies*, by which he means he acknowledges the role language plays in the constitution of subjectivity: 'But language is artifice. The human being is artificial. None of us is Rousseau Man, that noble savage, honest and untainted' (p. 184).

Winterson's anti-realism frequently finds expression in the dominant motif of flight as an image of escape which signifies freedom from the prison house of realist representation. This appears *inter alia* through Fortunata in *Sexing the Cherry*, through Sappho and Picasso in *Art & Lies* and through the pilot in the title story of *The World and Other Places*. The motif of flight also indicates the search for existential freedom: Winterson's heroes and heroines constantly seek to transgress boundaries and free themselves of constraints of various kinds. Through their fantastic journeys the reader vicariously acts out their own desire to cut loose. Love, too, is represented through images of weightlessness. In *Written* the narrator describes the beloved Louise as the 'winged horse Pegasus' (p. 132), and in *The PowerBook* the narrator states, 'Our happiness will be like the flight of birds' (p. 204). But, as Winterson asks in *Weight*, 'How many of us ever get free of our orbit?' (p. 99). And, for every character such as Villanelle or Fortunata, there is a character such as Jordan or Atlas who is forced to acknowledge that 'it is hard for anyone to change anything' (p. 99). Indeed, all Winterson's work revolves around this central tension between responsibility and freedom, weight and weightlessness, commitment and restless desire; and what she calls 'the same old story – boundaries, desire' (W, p. 131) forms the constant thread in her oeuvre.

STRUCTURE OF THE BOOK

Chapter 2, concluding Part I, provides a biographical reading of Winterson's life including her highly religious Lancashire childhood with adoptive parents, her writing career beginning with the publication of her first novel, and the subsequent media interest in her life. It considers her status as a public figure, her varied interests in and contributions to British cultural life, and the self-proclaimed tensions in her life between her work and her relationships. Finally, it discusses the ways in which she reworks her own experience imaginatively, drawing on multiple genres and discourses in the process.

In Part II, I discuss Winterson's major works from the 1980s, 1990s and 2000s. Chapter 3 discusses *Oranges Are Not the Only Fruit* (1985), *The Passion* (1987) and *Sexing the Cherry* (1989), examining their striking and innovative use of magic realism and the fantastic in the context of postmodernism. The dominant features of her work in this period are youthful idealism, an optimistic outlook and an exuberant use of language. This writing is characterized by metaphors of light, flight and weightlessness. Winterson establishes her central themes from this period as love, storytelling and the exploration of gender and sexuality. Her first novel, *Oranges Are Not the Only Fruit* (1985), is treated as an innovative lesbian reworking of the Bildungsroman, which nevertheless eschews the signifier 'lesbian'. *The Passion* (1987) and *Sexing the Cherry* (1989) are discussed as examples of 'historical' fiction which both interrogate (what is meant by) and intervene in history.

Chapter 4 considers how in the 1990s Winterson turns to science as a metaphor to explore love, art and human desire in works that are distinctly more sombre and introspective than her exuberant 1980s texts. *Written on the Body* (1992), *Art & Lies* (1994) and *Gut Symmetries* (1997) share a central metaphor of the body as text and undertake a simultaneous celebration and demystification of romantic love. They are among Winterson's most experimental and challenging works: *Written* experiments with a narrator of indeterminate gender, while *Art & Lies* pushes the novel form to its limits. The chapter also examines the contradictions and paradoxes that have increasingly emerged in Winterson's work of the 1990s, notably her ongoing commitment to anti-realist and postmodern stylistics and her simultaneous investment in love, art and the imagination as transcendent values.

The 2000s saw Winterson carrying her investigation of the interrelationship between science and human culture into the terrains of information technology, evolutionary theory and mythology. In Chapter 5, my analysis of *The PowerBook* (2000), *Lighthousekeeping* (2004) and *Weight* (2005) addresses Keulks's claim that these works can be read as 'artistic signposts . . . of her shifting relationship to both realism and postmodernism' (2007, p. 147), both stretching the postmodern aesthetic to its limits and appearing to draw back from its more relativistic implications. In *The PowerBook* (2000) Winterson utilizes virtual reality as a metaphor for a utopian fictional realm in which the meanings of gender, sexuality and the body may be transformed. I examine how she employs the disembodied mode of writing to represent the body as variously male and female, heterosexual and queer. In the context of a decade of ambivalent critical responses to her work, and in the light of her own admission that with *The PowerBook* she came to the end of a seven-book cycle, the chapter also analyses her 2004 novel, *Lighthousekeeping*, as a turning point in her writing career. On one hand, it represents both a continuation and an extension of her familiar themes of the multiplicity of identity and reality; on the other, it represents a move away from the thoroughgoing postmodernism of earlier works. In *Weight* Winterson reworks Greek mythology to explore philosophical issues about the meaning of life. As the novel's introduction attests, the themes of 'loneliness, responsibility, burden and freedom' (p. viii) are emerging as the dominant concerns of Winterson's work in the 2000s.

In Part III, following a short interview with the author discussing her recent work in Chapter 6, Chapter 7 considers Winterson's prolific and varied non-fiction and other writings including her journalism, her collection of essays, *Art Objects: Essays on Ecstasy and Effrontery*, and her children's books, *The King of Capri* and *Tanglewreck*. It discusses the critically acclaimed early adaptation of her first novel for BBC TV, and the stage adaptation of *The PowerBook* by Deborah Warner. In addition, the chapter examines Winterson's interest in cyber technologies, the dissemination of her work on the Internet and the role her website plays for her many web-based fans. Finally, Chapter 8 provides a comprehensive review of the critical reception of Winterson's work, treating the variety of theoretical paradigms which have informed it. The chapter highlights both her work's perceived strengths and shortcomings, and discusses the way in which criticism of her writing and persona often overlap. The study concludes with selected works by Jeanette Winterson and a complete list of works cited.

2

A BIOGRAPHICAL READING

I prefer myself as a character in my own fiction.

(*Art Objects*, p. 53)

In a recent interview with the author, Kate Kellaway comments,

She has been written about so much – and has written about herself so much, above all in her celebrated autobiographical first novel *Oranges Are Not the Only Fruit* (1985), that it is easy to feel, without having met her, that Jeanette Winterson is a known quantity. Easy – but a mistake.

(2006, online)

Winterson would no doubt approve of this assessment, not only because it warns against a too easy elision of life and art, but because it suggests that she retains the ability to surprise an audience. The facts of her early life are well known: Jeanette Winterson was born in Manchester on 27 August 1959 and afterwards adopted and brought up by a working-class couple in Accrington, Lancashire. From an early age she attended a Pentecostal church with her devoutly religious mother whose ambition was for Jeanette to become a missionary. In a highly unconventional childhood, described accurately in her first novel *Oranges Are Not the Only Fruit*, Winterson preached the gospel from the age of eight and wrote sermons, which she described as 'good exercise for writing precise prose' (Cooper, 1986). She attended Accrington Girls' Grammar School but was not encouraged to be intellectual or read widely. Indeed, her mother proscribed outside reading material at home and her father only 'read' only the *Beano*. Winterson reports that there were only six books in the family home, two of which were bibles (*AO*, p. 153). Her early exposure to biblical language gave her the sense of 'language as something holy' (*ibid*.). and produced a lasting 'positive, creative effect' on her which informs all her writing. She has commented that the Bible represents 'the beginning text for me for everything that happens' (Miller, 2005, p. 11). In addition, she read Malory's *Morte d'Arthur*, another text which 'started her life quest of reading and writing' (personal website, 2007). A Saturday job at the public library gave her access to books, which she had to keep hidden from her mother's censorious gaze beneath her mattress and read in the outside toilet, her peculiarly working-class version of a 'room of one's own' (*AO*, p. 153). Books were clearly Winterson's salvation long before she became a published writer. She has described them eloquently as 'flying carpets', enabling her to escape an unhappy childhood (Winterson, '*Saturday Live*', 2007).

At 16 Winterson, like her fictional counterpart in *Oranges*, fell in love with another girl. The rift with her mother and Church community forced her to leave home and move in temporarily with her English teacher. She spent the next few years supporting herself at a variety of jobs in the North West including ice-cream seller, an undertaker's assistant and a domestic in a mental hospital. She did her 'A' Levels at Accrington College of Further Education, and spent many hours in the public library, before applying to read English at Oxford, which represented a 'fairy tale' place in her imagination (Miller, 2005, p. 11). According to Winterson, she was originally turned down but camped in the city until St Catherine's College finally gave her a place (*ibid*.). She now says that the university experience toughened her up – one tutor apparently greeted her friend Vicky Licorish and Winterson as follows: 'You are the black experiment and you are the working class experiment' (Edemariam, 2007, online). After graduating in 1981, Winterson moved to London and worked briefly in advertising before taking a job at the Roundhouse theatre. In 1983 at the age of 24 Winterson began writing her first novel. The following year, she became an editor at Brilliance Books and then Pandora, where she met Phillippa Brewster, who published *Oranges Are Not the Only Fruit* in 1985. A second book, the comic novel *Boating for Beginners*, came out soon afterwards, followed by *The Passion* in 1987 and

Sexing the Cherry in 1989. By the end of the decade, Winterson had become an established and widely acclaimed author on the British literary scene. At the same time, she also began producing work in a range of other media, including journalism, radio plays, film scripts and screen adaptations of her work (see Chapter 7). Highlights include the critically acclaimed BBC television film version of *Oranges* in 1990, which won a BAFTA and the Prix D'Argent at Cannes, and her 2002 stage version of *The PowerBook*, which was performed at the National Theatre in London and Théâtre de Chaillot in Paris. She has also written books for children, has had a number of regular broadsheet columns and maintains a lively personal website, which receives approximately 20,000 hits per month and which she is rightly proud of, saying, 'I have to throw some money at it and make it sexy' (Winterson, '*Saturday Live*', 2007).

By 2008, with 18 books to her name, Winterson has amassed an impressive body of work for someone still comparatively young. As she is the first to admit, she has made an extremely good living from her writing and sales of her work remain strong. She represents a comparatively rare figure, the literary writer with a popular following. In 1992 Winterson formed her own company, Great Moments Inc., to handle her work, and by the end of the 1990s she was earning approximately £250,000, 'putting her among the top 50 English writers in terms of earning power' (Lambert, 1998, online). Her then editor, Frances Coady, reported that advances of £150,000 were justified given Winterson's importance as a writer and the fact that she 'occupies very unusual and difficult ground, being both literary and commercial' (*ibid.*). In the 2006 Honours List she was awarded the OBE. In 2007 Winterson published *The Stone Gods*, an interesting work of speculative fiction which has been generally well received by the critics. She is also working on a new novel for children, to be published by Bloomsbury in 2008. She would also like to collaborate with Deborah Warner and write a libretto, perhaps based on her novella *Weight* (Kellaway, 2006). In a recent Radio 4 *Saturday Live* broadcast, Winterson was asked by Fi Glover what she would wish for as her legacy. She replied, 'My work, because it's the best of me.' Her hope is 'to prompt some kind of emotional and imaginative change in people' (Winterson, *Saturday Live*, 2007). Clearly the days of passionate preaching have not been forgotten.

Winterson's career has not always run smoothly, however, and has often reflected the perceived vicissitudes of her personal life. Open and honest about her sexuality in interviews from the start of her career, Winterson has had to negotiate the press and public's prurient interest in her relationships with women to a greater extent than would be the case for a heterosexual writer. In the early days of her success, Winterson no doubt cultivated the 'wild girl' image which circulated about her and her supposedly numerous love affairs became legendary in press coverage. Although she has admitted playing up to her Lothario image, joking about trading sexual favours for saucepans, for example, she denies that what she did was 'prostitution' (Lambert, 1998) or that she had a 'bevy' of women attending on her during her Hampstead years in the early 1990s (Jaggi, 2004, online). The coverage undoubtedly damaged her reputation as a serious writer even as it demonstrated both the sexual double standards applied to women writers and the latent homophobia of the media. As Angela Lambert comments, 'many male authors behave far worse and their behaviour is indulgently seen as high spirits' (1998, online).

In fact Winterson has had significant relationships with three women: first, with the literary agent Pat Kavanagh (on which *Written on the Body* was partly based); secondly, with her partner of 13 years until 2001, the academic and radio broadcaster Margaret (Peggy) Reynolds; and most recently with the theatre director Deborah Warner, her present girlfriend. The pair does not live together, and Winterson has said of their relationship that

> I am very solitary about work. I need long tracts of time when I don't see anybody and can just be by myself. [. . .] You get a weekend here and there but that is fine. We don't need each other in that daily domestic way – and I don't think either of us could do it.
>
> (Kellaway, 2006)

As this suggests, Winterson views family life as inimical to the work of the artist. In interview she comments, 'I never work in a domestic space – the work is anti-social and messes up meal-times' (Winterson, *Guardian* online, 2000). In *Written on the Body*, the narrator observes, 'I don't want to reproduce, I want to make something entirely new' (p. 109), which may be interpreted in terms of both literary and sexual innovation.

In a fascinating interview with Libby Brooks, she stated that her lesbianism is a choice:

> It's very fashionable at the moment to say that everything is genetic, but it's a choice that I made quite consciously. I don't have any problems going to bed with men, don't dislike it, don't dislike them. I could choose, and with women I was able to get on with my life and do my work, and I'm not sure that I would have been able to do that if I'd been heterosexual. I feel like I didn't make a problem for myself, I made a solution.
>
> (Brooks, 2000, online)

This viewpoint aligns Winterson with the position of political lesbians who choose to direct their energy towards themselves and other women. It is also reminiscent of the choices made by Winterson's literary foremothers such as Virginia Woolf, who chose writing lives over motherhood. In 'Professions for Women', Woolf criticized the sexual ideology that limited women to domesticity and exhorted them to 'kill the angel in the house'. Winterson makes a similar link with feminism, calling femininity a construct, and stating that 'it's still difficult for women to express themselves in the way that men can, without any regard for what's happening around them' (Brooks, 2000).

While Winterson says that she does not regret not having children, that they would make her lifestyle impossible (Kellaway, 2006), she is part of an extended family which revolves around her two god-daughters, the children of television producer and actress Vicky Licorish, a close friend from Oxford days. Winterson sees the girls every second weekend, pays for their schooling and takes them on holiday. 'It's enriched my life completely, and I'm really glad', she stated recently (Edemariam, 2007). Winterson has successfully established in life something her characters strive for – loving bonds beyond the family: 'We have broken the nuclear family, which is a good thing', she comments (*ibid.*). She recently wrote of the scandal of children being abandoned in children's homes, suggesting that it would be cheaper for the state to send them to public school and let people such as herself 'adopt' some of them during the holidays (personal website, 2007).

Over the years, media coverage of her lifestyle and attitudes has led Winterson into the defensive position of de-emphasizing sexuality in an understandable effort to mitigate press obsession with the issue. Asked by a fan whether she was tired of being asked about her sexual preference, she replied, 'Yes! The British are obsessed with who you sleep with and how much you earn. I am published in twenty four countries, and only in the UK is there this mad obsession with bed and bits' (*Guardian* online, 2000). The essays in *Art Objects* express her views formed during the 1990s in reaction to the media representation of her life. When she writes, 'Art must resist autobiography if it hopes to cross boundaries of class, culture, and sexuality' (*AO*, p. 106), it is easy to read her frustration with questions about her personal life. While acknowledging the importance of gay and lesbian subcultures, she resists the identification of her work as lesbian fiction, stating emphatically that 'literature is not a lecture delivered to a special interest group' (p. 106), which echoes the views expressed in my interview with her (see Chapter 6). In a recent article for the *Evening Standard*, Winterson wrote a cogent critique of media heterosexism, stating that

> It is a pity to be labelled at all. I have never called myself a lesbian writer, and I would hate to be one. I am a writer. I have a girlfriend. My friends are not 'either' gay or straight, they are fun, interesting people, some with children, some not. To me, that's normal life. What is not normal, what is deeply abnormal, is our forensic fascination with gayness.
>
> (personal website, 2007)

Clearly, then, Winterson wants to claim her place in the mainstream of British culture rather than pursue a romance with the margins.

While critics routinely fasten on Winterson's lesbianism, her class background is just as important in defining who and what she has become. It is still the case that the majority of respected British writers are white, middle-class males notwithstanding the increasing numbers of women and black writers. Frances Coady, Winterson's one-time editor at Granta, agrees that some of the criticism derives from the fact that 'she's northern, she's originally working class and she's a lesbian, and so on all those counts she's a sitting duck, an alien species, for all those Oxbridge boys on newspapers' (Lambert, 1998). Winterson sees her achievement as 'exceptional' in class terms. Although more working-class writers have succeeded in the post-war period than previously, she views class as a crucial determinant of a person's life chances and expectations. In a 1998 interview she voiced her annoyance with middle-class people who think of themselves as underprivileged,

> when they have no idea what it means to run out of money on Wednesday and not get paid until Friday and not have a bank account and not have a telephone and not have a car and not know anybody who's got any of those things [. . .] these are the things that really separate people out [. . .] I don't know anybody – anybody – from my background who has been able or has wanted to cross the bridge into my kind of life.
>
> (Lambert, 1998)

Such forthright views have set her at odds with sections of the media with whom she has had a troubled relationship. During the 1990s, when in her thirties, Winterson went through an extremely difficult period, both personally and professionally, which she now refers to as her 'dark days' (Jaggi, 2004). The bad press for *Written on the Body* was accompanied by press attacks on her 'ill-mannered and arrogant' attitude by journalists to whom she had given short shrift. Indeed, Winterson is reported to have thrown one journalist out of her house for snooping and turned up on the doorstep of another to harangue her over an article in which she felt her integrity as a writer was being called into question (Lambert, 1998). The critical mauling affected her badly; she reportedly felt great self-loathing and close to mental collapse, as she admitted in a 2004 interview: 'I didn't know I could ever find my voice again; I thought I was destroyed. My writing used to be a place of joy and became a place of terror; I couldn't bear that' (Jaggi, 2004, online). In retrospect, as Winterson ruefully admits, she brought some of her misfortune on herself: 'About 1992 I should have had an operation to sew up my mouth, and kept it closed until 1997 [. . .] You can't make more of a mess of it than I did. I went mad and behaved like an idiot' (*ibid.*). It is impossible to read the lines, spoken by the character Handel, in her poorly received 1994 novel *Art & Lies* without thinking of Winterson's own 'dark night of the soul': 'Isn't this life Hell enough?' (p. 113). While Winterson has come to terms with this period and is able to discuss it in interviews, she does so in 'the language of fairy tale', no doubt as a way of distancing it and registering its foreignness (Miller, 2005, p. 11).

Given her reception over the years, she is understandably wary of journalists. Like many 'celebrities', Winterson has been forced to develop a more sustainable relationship with the media, as a result of which her profile is now much improved. Commenting on the cultural trend towards treating writers as celebrities, Winterson believes it is regrettable but probably inevitable: 'My own view is to cooperate now as much as I can and to try and keep private what I can' (Winterson, 'Appendix', 2005, p. 7). In 2004 she stated, 'I'm lucky I have a fantastic life. I've found it again, like coming back from the dead' (Jaggi, 2004). As she approaches 50, Winterson has developed a relaxed and affable public persona, met with enthusiasm by audiences, demonstrated in a recent edition of Radio 4's *Saturday Live* (2007) in which she engaged in friendly banter with the show's presenter Fi Glover.

The new millennium proved a turning point for the author, her books greeted with interest if not universal acclaim. Winterson describes having reached the end of a cycle: 'In my subconscious, those books were part of a single emotional journey, and *The PowerBook* was a summation; a gaudy, baroque, extravagant book, packing in everything I'd learned and felt since *Oranges*; crossing time, altering gender, refusing linear connections. I'd found myself and I'd found my voice again' (Jaggi, 2004). Her split from Reynolds came not long after her move to London from the Cotswolds, where she owns a seventeenth-century cottage. Her main home is an eighteenth-century Huguenot house in Spitalfields, which she has restored beautifully from a ruined state. The Spitalfields house appears in the 'meatspace' section of *The PowerBook*, identified by the old shop sign 'Verde', which in actuality also reads 'J & W Fruit'. Indeed, in keeping with the house's commercial past, and in response to an unwelcome offer from Starbucks, she opened an independent grocer's shop there in 2000. Commentators sometimes express surprise at Winterson's commercial nous, but considering her working-class background and the fact that she worked from the age of nine in a market stall, it is no surprise that Winterson has proved herself an accomplished businesswoman. The Spitalfields house is on the tourist trail of various London walks, both in its own right and because of its famous resident. Rather rueing this aspect of fame, Winterson neverthe-less likes the hustle and bustle of the area, writing in *The PowerBook* about the layers of history of the house and the surrounding area and, significantly, its importance as a place of refuge.

As her latest novel about a planet which dies through exhaus-tion demonstrates, Winterson is concerned about climate change and 'does her bit' to be green. She has installed a geo-thermal heating system at her house. However, she also ruefully admits to loving cars – she owns a Porsche – and argues that one must 'balance the party against responsibility' ('*Saturday Live*', 2007). As this suggests, Winterson's personality embraces contradictions, a point also made by numerous interviewers who have commented that she is a striking combination of self-confidence and shyness, defiance and vulnerability (Jaggi, 2004). The former Winterson attributes to her religious training and the latter to working-class diffidence towards the chattering classes. In a recent interview Winterson drew a characteristically defiant and disarming self-portrait: 'If I was a dog, I'd be a terrier. I was brought up in quite a tough culture – I'm used to speaking out' (Kellaway, 2006). As interviews with friends and colleagues attest, Winterson is intensely loyal to those close to her and clearly inspires loyalty in her friends, many of whom have known her since the early days of her career. Her friend Philippa Giles, the television producer, describes her warmly as 'honest, forthright, generous', but also 'naive' and childlike (*ibid.*). Another friend, and fellow writer, Ali Smith calls Winterson 'brave and courageous' and ascribes to her a 'charisma', which is 'left over from her preaching days' (*ibid.*). What emerges is a portrait of someone who is fiercely self-reliant and self-creating, pushing herself on to experience life intensely, yet whose passionate and impulsive nature maintains strong links to the world of childhood. Elsewhere, Winterson has described herself as a natural optimist, a lover of good food and as enor-mously energetic: 'a ferret with a firework strapped to my back' ('*Saturday Live*', 2007), which is presumably the reason she never appears to put on weight. She told listeners of a recent Radio 4 pro-gramme her star sign (Virgo) and that she liked doing the laundry (*ibid.*).

But of course there is another side to the 'child of nature': Win-terson the intellectual. Notwithstanding her working-class back-ground and Lancashire accent, Winterson's conversation is full of literary allusions and she speaks knowledgably on a wide range of cultural topics as the author interview in Chapter 6 attests. In the same Radio 4 programme, Winterson also discussed her love of opera, listing her favourite song as Maria Callas singing the aria from *Tosca*, 'I live for Art, I live for Love.' In *Art Objects*, Winterson describes her adult education in and growing passion for the visual arts. Indeed, Winterson is a collector of both modern art and first editions of her favourite books: she owns several signed copies of Woolf's works including *A Room of One's Own* and *Orlando*.[1] Other favourite works, listed in an interview she gave for the paperback edition of *Lighthousekeeping*, include T.S. Eliot's *Four Quartets* (which she describes as both her favourite poem and the most important of the twentieth century); *Invisible Cities* by Italo Calvino; *The Inferno* by Dante; and *Venice* by the travel writer Jan Morris. Winterson has described her affinity with the metaphysical poets, particularly John Donne, and their use of language. She particularly admires the modernist writers T.S. Eliot and Virginia Woolf, Eliot for his invention of new forms and treatment of time, and Woolf for her creation of new possibilities in language (Miller, 2005, p. 11). Through her relationship with Peggy Reynolds, she has had first-hand experience of the work of literary historians and has a deep respect for what she sees as real work. She is of course an accomplished literary critic herself, as her book of essays *Art Objects* attests. Her readings of Woolf's *Orlando* and the work of Gertrude Stein are energetic and insightful. Her impressively wide knowledge of Western literature also informs her fiction, which draws on sources as diverse as the medieval tradition of romance to the poems of Muriel Rukeyser.

Winterson's attitude to popular culture has on the whole been a negative one, particularly in the 1990s. She sees much of it as intellectually unchallenging and of limited value: 'I do not care about fashion, only about permanencies' (*AO*, p. 5) and she makes a firm distinction between real art and fake media (p. 15). Her novel *Art & Lies* in particular presented a coruscating attack on 'cultural relativists' and populists. It is hard to disentangle Winterson's justified dismay at the cultural decline of Britain in the 1990s from her personal feeling of being critically mocked and 'left out in the cold' at this stage in her career. More recently, her newspaper columns have taken a more moderate and humorous glance at popular culture. Nevertheless, it is to true to say that despite the playful postmodern style of much of her fiction, Winterson has consistently placed herself in the modernist tradition of promoting what is challenging and 'difficult', the so-called High Art. She is dismissive of the best-selling popular genres of 'lad lit' and 'chick lit', criticizing the 'middle class bad boys' with their 'blunt prose' and the 'copycat girls who wouldn't know one end of a dildo from a vacuum rod' (AO, p. 114). Such criticisms make sense in the context of Winterson's quasi-religious attitude to books, which she describes as 'doors': 'you open them and they take you through to another world' ('*Saturday Live*', 2007).

Winterson is a writer who fiercely defends the distinction between art and the everyday, seeing the former as a privileged realm. To questions about the autobiographical character of her work, she responds, 'There is no such thing as autobiography. There is only art and lies' (AL, p. 141). In the introduction to *Weight* she explains, 'Of course I wrote it out of my own situation. There is no other way' (p. xviii). She insists that the concept of autobiography is a misnomer; what is important is to convey a sense of authenticity: 'I believe there is always exposure, vulnerability in the writing process, which is not to say it is either confessional or memoir. Simply, it is real' (p. xix). And in *The PowerBook*, she writes, 'The fixed part [of biography] is only a base camp – the journeys out from there are what interests' (p. 215). Repeatedly Winterson rejects the authorial fallacy, whether this takes the form of arguing that the author's life is irrelevant to an appreciation of their art (AO, p. 27) or insisting on the intertextual character of identity. At one point in *The PowerBook*, Ali says admiringly of Rembrandt: 'No artist had so conspicuously made himself both the subject and the object of his work' (p. 214). As Peter Childs observes, 'this is something that could be said of Winterson; not that her writing is extraordinarily autobiographical but that she is intimately concerned with the emotions and feelings of the individual self, which are revealed and scrutinized, displayed and studied' (2005, pp. 260–261).

Despite her disclaimers about autobiography, the adult Winterson appears frequently in her fiction through her various alter egos, doppelgangers and mouthpieces; the tone of her voice, especially in the philosophical, metafictional sections of the texts, is unmistakeable. Compare, for example, the nameless narrator of *Written* with the emailer Ali/Alix in *The PowerBook*. At one point, *Written*'s narrator adopts the Winterson persona of numerous interviews: 'I don't lack self-confidence but I'm not beautiful' (p. 85). As Susana Onega points out,

> Strikingly echoing Pound's poet as wandering Odysseus, then, Winterson presents herself as a mythical quester cutting across the boundaries of her own books and knitting them together by means of slightly differing repetitions of recurrent themes or *leitmotifs*, in an attempt to unify individual works into a single art object that may be said to have the shape of Winterson's own process of artistic or spiritual maturation.
>
> (2006, p. 7)

She also consciously weaves herself and the people she knows into the fabric of her fiction in the belief that identity is in an important sense fictional and that it is through stories that we come to understand ourselves most fully (*AO*, p. 59). Her novel *Art & Lies* presents a metacommentary on the relationship between art and life, in which the narrator poses the challenging question 'What can be known about me?' (p. 137). All her work demonstrates an awareness of both the slipperiness of language and its power to create identity: 'I speak therefore I am', she writes in *Art & Lies*; 'by my words you will know me' (p. 138), in which the authorial voice appears to speak directly to the reader. At one point, Handel conceives of himself as a parrot – 'I know I am made up of other people's say-so' (p. 184). Winterson appears to both register anxiety about the originality of her own words and ruefully acknowledge the critics and commentators, busily making her up in accounts such as this one.

Winterson's work draws extensively on her personal experience of both family life and sexual relationships. Winterson is unapologetic about the fact that her former lovers, Pat Kavanagh and Peggy Reynolds, have made thinly disguised appearances in her work, appearing as Louise in *Written on the Body*, Stella in *Gut Symmetries*, and every other red-haired, pre-Raphaelite beauty in Winterson's fiction. Sexual love is of course Winterson's big topic. Some critics seem embarrassed about Winterson's disclosures and see her, in consequence, as fair game for prurient questions. In *Art & Lies* she appears, ruefully, to acknowledge this, speaking in the voice of Sappho: 'I do have a lot to answer for, all those imaginary seductions in the flesh and on the page' (p. 69). Yet, as Kellaway attests, 'She has never stopped trying to unriddle love: *The Passion, Sexing the Cherry, Written on the Body* are all romantic crusades. And Winterson's lesbian identity is essential to this: she writes with the zeal of a St George liberating a princess from the dragon's mouth' (Kellaway, 2000, online).

Another prominent theme in her work, the nature of the mother–child relationship, draws on Winterson's relationship with her adopted mother. Indeed Mrs Winterson exists as a textual presence throughout her work: *Oranges* provides the oft-cited example, but she also appears in the 'Muck House' sections of *The PowerBook* and *Lighthousekeeping*. The story told by Mother Muck is closely based on Winterson's biographical experience and is reworked in her children's novel *Tanglewreck* as well as *Oranges*. All these works contain poignant, confessional passages, in which the author-narrator attributes the lack of parental love to her questing nature and longing for love. In a recent radio interview, Winterson talked about Mrs Winterson's 'monstrous qualities' (*Saturday Live*, 2007). These emerge repeatedly in her work, represented in the grotesque features and attributes of power and violence of her maternal figures from Lou in *Oranges* to Mrs Rockabye in *Tanglewreck*, 'who only ever quoted the nastier bits of the Bible' (p. 123). Similarly, in *Weight*, Winterson ascribes her own 'Atlas complex' to the experience of being rejected by two mothers. She writes that 'as a character in my own fiction, I had a chance to escape the facts' (p. 139), which echoes her desire, stated repeatedly in interviews, that she writes to become 'the hero of my own life' ('*Saturday Live*', 2007). In an extra-diegetic section the author-narrator considers how her origins have shaped her attitude to life:

> I know nothing of my biological parents. They live on a lost continent of DNA. Like Atlantis all record of them is sunk. They are guesswork, speculation, mythology. The only proof I have of them is myself, and what proof is that, so many times written over? Written on the body is a secret code, only visible in certain lights. I do not know my time of birth. I am not entirely sure of the date. Having brought no world with me, I made one.
>
> (*W*, p. 141)

She talks about her anger, her 'red-hot forest' and how 'I try not to burn up my world with rage' (p. 142). For Winterson, therefore, fiction writing, 'telling the story again', becomes an escape route – 'I could invent myself out of the world' (p. 139); 'My journeys were a matter of survival' (p. 138) and a form of self-invention and self-determination.

While her heroines, like herself, are childless, Winterson discovers a connection with children in her art by writing frequently from the child's perspective. This can be seen most clearly in Winterson's series of girl child narrators in *Oranges, Gut Symmetries, Lighthousekeeping* and *Tanglewreck*, who continue a process of feminizing the Bildungsroman genre and recreating the origin stories of women. In a recent interview Winterson made explicit her identification with the various child personae in her fiction, including the most recent, the character Silver in *Tanglewreck*:

> Silver is me. She is a continuation of the me that sits inside *Oranges*. She is an only child, self-inventing. [. . .] She makes herself up but she is also making up the world because she doesn't trust what is out there, or it is not reliable, or there is a problem that only she can solve. That is the push of the book.
>
> (Kellaway, 2006)

As Winterson's unique biographical intertextuality attests, many of the major tropes in her work have their echo if not their origins in Winterson's life. Perhaps the central one which pervades her work is the metaphor of flight as liberation or escape – from material burdens or unhappiness. In *Art & Lies*, she writes, 'But I dream of flight, not to be as the angels are, but to rise above the smallness that I am. Against the daily death the iconography of wings' (p. 114). Drawing on but rejecting the religious connotations of the motif, Winterson characteristically turns a potentially self-aggrandizing image ('to be as the angels are') into a self-deprecating one ('the smallness that I am'), transforming it into poetry ('the iconography of wings'). One set of constraints that both her life and her work seek to break free of is that of gender. Replying to a question about the centrality of gender in her work, Winterson responds, 'Gender is a template, a beginning, a set of possibilities, it's not a rigid structure and should never be a prison. I'm interested in gender play not gender roles' (*Guardian* online, 2000).

Comments such as this have encouraged several generations of feminist readers, critics and students of her work. Yet Winterson's attitude to academic criticism is an ambivalent one. Miller reports that 'feminist criticism often irritates her' as being too doctrinaire (Miller, 2005, p. 11). Given the choice between a 'political' and a 'humanist' reading of Donne's 'O, my America, my new found land', she would 'go for the sexy, romantic reading' (*ibid*.). She seems, by turns, flattered and irritated by the attentions of students and theorists of her work. The website run by Anna Troberg[2] has been visited by adoring fans writing papers on her novels. In a *Guardian*-sponsored discussion with fans, she admitted to finding Cixous 'fabulous', but insisted that 'creative work influences theory and not the other way round' (*Guardian* online, 2000). Asked about the connection between desires of the body and the writing she uses to describe them, Winterson responds, with a seeming endorsement of the theories of écriture féminine:

> All of my work is pumped through my body. I live very directly, without much split between heart and head. Physical things inform my thinking. It's inevitable that this attitude or nature informs my work. I don't think art is a head thing, I think it's a total experience, and one identified by emotion.
>
> (*Guardian* online, 2000)

Winterson has sometimes been criticized for eschewing a realistic engagement with contemporary social issues (Showalter, 2000, online) and for privileging fantastic or interior worlds. However, writing in her September 2007 website column, just prior to the publication of *The Stone Gods*, Winterson addressed the issue of the artist's relationship to her society, stating that

> I believe that the role of the artist changes, according to the time that he or she must inhabit. I have felt strongly that in our time, the inner life, the imaginative life, the life of the mind, needed strengthening and protection, because we live so much on the outside, pretending that all our needs can be met by a bit more shopping and technology. I have never been much interested in naturalistic writing – a kind of printed version of TV dramas, and I have tried to use the exactness of heightened poetic language to prompt thought and to make new connections . . .
>
> (personal website, 2007)

While justifying her rejection of naturalism in favour of her characteristic dense poetic prose, she nevertheless registers the need for a more direct approach to 'the state of the world', calling her new novel a 'response to where we are now, and where this now may be taking us' (*ibid*.). As an artist, she is not 'giving up anything I have done [. . .] but I am bringing in something else, something more. All we can do is to try and make a difference' (*ibid*.).

Winterson's most recent works develop her concerns about global and environmental destruction. She reports that her god-daughters are 'worried about the planet' (Edemariam, 2007) and feels it is time to address the issue in her own work. In a recent interview she commented that 'things were now so urgent, so disturbing in the world, and I'd reached a particular point where I felt I had to step in, and use whatever I could to make a statement about that' (*ibid*.). In particular, she wants to examine how, in her view, 'technology is taking over science, how mechanistic it is. Without wishing to be too polemical, I wanted to challenge people's ideas about what science can do' (Else and Harris, 2007, online). These comments attest yet again both to Winterson's belief in the power of fiction and her own sense of mission. To charges that Winterson is doom-mongering, she replies, 'I don't want to sound a doom-monger because I'm not one. I'm optimistic. I do feel we have every chance, but not unless we are realistic, both about our own negativity and our own possibility' (*ibid*.).

While Winterson has thought of herself as a writer for as long as she can remember, she characterizes her writing talent in distinctly religious terms as an 'act of grace', one that she does not take for granted, admitting that the writing process has become more rather than less difficult as time passes: 'I throw a lot away', she comments (Miller, 2005, p. 11). Regarding her legacy, she states, 'I'm not worried about posterity, just about the work I'm doing each day and whether it is the best I can do' (*ibid*.). As a perfectionist who sets herself very high standards, one suspects that Winterson cares intensely about 'posterity'. As her work attests, Winterson has redirected her moral sense towards literature, asserting her belief in the restorative and transformative powers of literature. Like Matthew Arnold, Winterson believes in its salvational qualities: books really did change her life.

Part II
MAJOR WORKS

3

ORANGES ARE NOT THE ONLY FRUIT, THE PASSION AND *SEXING THE CHERRY*

REWRITING THE BILDUNGSROMAN: *ORANGES ARE NOT THE ONLY FRUIT* (1985)

As everyone who has read the novel knows, *Oranges Are Not the Only Fruit* relates the story of Jeanette, a young girl adopted by an evangelical couple in a Lancashire Mill Town in the 1960s. In a vivid first-person narrative, stretching from the age of seven to twenty one, Jeanette recounts the frequently comic and poignant experiences that befall her with a mixture of innocence and know-ingness. Initially an enthusiastic religious preacher, Jeanette is forced to leave the Church when she falls in love with another girl. This leads to a breach with her mother and she leaves home to make her own way in the world. After working in a variety of jobs she gains a place at Oxford University; and the novel ends with a visit home and a partial reconciliation with her mother. *Oranges* also includes inset fairy tales and philosophical reflections on history and storytelling.

The novel's depiction of growing up different in a North of England town was read in two main ways: in the mainstream press, as a funny, poignant story of self-discovery, stressing 'universal' themes and only incidentally about a working-class lesbian; and in the feminist press, as a challenge to the oppressive patriarchal institutions of Church and family and a positive assertion of lesbian identity (Hinds, 1992). Thereafter the novel's semantic richness opened a variety of readings foregrounding its use of magic realism and postmodern metafiction. Laura Doan (1994) set the critical tone in an influential essay identifying Winterson's aim as challenging and deconstructing a range of grand narratives including oppressive gender binaries. Notwithstanding the novel's realist and autobiographical aspects, Winterson gave her imprimatur to this postmodern reading, presenting it as anti-linear and spiral in her introduction to the paperback edition. As Winterson's first text, it is tempting to provide an account of *Oranges* as a typical first novel which introduces both the themes of love and storytelling and the postmodern techniques which characterize her subsequent work. In addition to exploring these aspects of the novel, I want to place it in context, both historical and generic, viewing it as a specifically lesbian reworking of the Bildungsroman genre or novel of development. This has the effect of de-individualizing the work, in Michel Foucault's terms of suspending – albeit temporarily – the power of the author function, so that we see *Oranges* not simply as Winterson's engaging and unique work of magic realism, but as a striking – and in many ways innovative – contribution to a specific tradition of autobiographical storytelling.

The Bildungsroman genre conventionally inscribes a myth of origins, delineating the formation of the hero/heroine's identity. In examples of the female novel of development, from Charlotte Bronte's *Jane Eyre* to Sylvia Plath's *The Bell Jar*, the acquisition of selfhood is structured as a quest or journey in which the heroine must pass through a number of stages, in the process negotiating gender difference and heterosexual femininity. In the related genre of the Künstlerroman, the novel of the development of the artist, as Rachel Blau du Plessis demonstrates, the relationship between mother and daughter is central, and the romance plot is replaced by the story of a daughter becoming an artist 'to extend, reveal and elaborate her mother's thwarted talent' (1985, p. 93). In the case of the lesbian Bildungsroman, a prominent place is granted to the genesis and development of the *lesbian* subject. The genre depicts the protagonist's recognition of emotional and sexual feelings for women, her recognition that such feelings are taboo and illegitimate in her culture, and the way in which she deals with this understanding. In the modern genre this involves a psychological acceptance and public affirmation of her lesbianism.[1]

Following this model, *Oranges* begins with Jeanette's reconstruction of her origins. In common with other examples of the lesbian Bildungsroman, atypicality rather than representativeness is highlighted, and Jeanette is presented as 'special'. As she states in the appropriately titled first section 'Genesis', 'I cannot remember a time when I did not know that I was special' (p. 3). Difference is also signified by Winterson's chosen title which gestures metaphorically towards a different ontology. Winterson presents an exemplary narrative of extraordinary girlhood: Jeanette has an atypical home life in relation to the wider community; she is set apart from other children and feels different to them; she is unusually intelligent and has a strong sense of self; she is influenced by a strong maternal figure who is eccentric, domineering and zealous, and with whom she has a love/hate relationship. Ultimately, she expresses her difference by rejecting conventional femininity, thus making her a feminist heroine, and her unconventionality eventually finds positive expression in lesbianism.

The novel uses humour to portray, in the style of the picaresque, Jeanette's adventures as she negotiates family life and clashes with the values of the outside world. It depicts a series of comic episodes focusing on her eccentric and non-conformist childhood, which present girlhood as an almost surreal experience. The comedy is a product of her mother's attempts – and failures – to invent Jeanette in her own image. As the adopted daughter of a Pentecostal Evangelist, destined to become a missionary, Jeanette is perceived as one of 'the elect'. In fact, religion works in the first half of text as a metaphor for Jeanette's as yet unspoken sexual difference. It is only when she begins to acknowledge this publicly and to herself that the metaphor collapses and the two discourses – religious and sexual 'election' – come into explicit and painful conflict. Thus the foregrounding of atypicality partly works to mark out lesbian difference in the text, signifying an identity premised on a rebellion against normative heterosexual femininity.

Like the extraordinary girls depicted in the female Bildungsroman, Jeanette relates more easily to adults than to other children, whom she sees as virtually another species. Her mother imparts an esoteric knowledge that makes her appear monstrously precocious to outsiders. Demonstrating this knowledge is a source of pride to Jeanette, and a source of horror and alarm for her teachers such as when Jeanette stitches an Old Testament prophecy of doom into her biblical sampler. In another episode she grows a hyacinth for a competition and entitles it 'The Annunciation': 'This was because the blooms were huddled up close, and reminded me of Mary and Elisabeth soon after the visit by the angel. I thought it was a very clever marriage of horticulture and theology, but it didn't win' (p. 47). As the philosophical voice of the narrator's older self then remarks, 'what constitutes a problem is not the thing, or the environment where we find the thing, but the conjunction of the two' (p. 47). Jeanette's religious world view is deemed unnatural in a child by her liberal-minded teachers, but is commended by her mother who takes her to the cinema as a reward.

In Jeanette's working-class community women dominate private and public life, which is centred on the Church. Fathers are shadowy figures who barely feature at all. Jeanette even refers to her father as 'Mother's husband' and remarks, 'I thought he was nice although he didn't say much' (p. 36). Much of the novel's humour involves the depiction of a family life in which conventional gender expectations and roles are reversed:

Like most people I lived for a long time with my mother and father. My father liked to watch the wrestling, my mother like to wrestle; it didn't matter what. She was in the white corner and that was that.

(p. 1)

Many readers have commented on the lack of normative heterosexual role models in the text. Whereas in many examples of women's autobiographical fiction the heroine becomes aware that gender is mediated by possession or lack of the phallus, resulting in either disavowal or a version of penis envy, this is not the case in *Oranges*. Indeed, Jeanette does not so much disavow the phallus as fail to notice it: in her strongly matriarchal community 'men were something you had around the place, not particularly interesting, but quite harmless' (p. 127). On account of her prominent role in the Church, Jeanette never experiences the sense of gender inferiority common to many Bildungsroman heroines and her negotiation of gender difference is remarkably lacking in conflict. Indeed, as she remarks, 'in terms of power I had enough to keep Mussolini happy' (p. 124). Although Jeanette ultimately rejects the values of her mother and her community, she does not deny their role in shaping her identity and providing her with a strong, if not impregnable, sense of self. Through her mother she acquires the self-conviction, determination and power of prophecy, which sustain her as a lesbian and, we are led to believe, as an artist.

While *Oranges* shares the tendency of the lesbian Bildungsroman to represent the mother's domination of the protagonist's early years as somehow implicated in her development as a lesbian, it is too simplistic to suggest that *Oranges* represents Mrs Winterson as responsible for her daughter's lesbianism. Rather, she provides a model of indomitable female strength which the heroine carries over into her relationships, even as she reacts against the negative aspects of her mother's character. Interestingly, Winterson's depiction of the strong and supportive bonds between women finds a striking resonance in a key theoretical work from the period, in which the poet and critic Adrienne Rich articulated a new model of lesbian existence based on a shared female identity:

> I mean the term *lesbian continuum* to include a range – through each woman's life and throughout history – of woman-identified experience, not simply the fact that a woman has had or consciously desired sexual experience with another woman. If we expand it to embrace many more forms of primary intensity between and among women, including the sharing of a rich inner life, the bonding against male tyranny, the giving and receiving of practical and political support . . . we begin to grasp breadths of female history which have lain out of reach . . . .
>
> (1993, p. 239)

Like Rich, Winterson's text seeks to distinguish lesbian selfhood from the clinical and limiting concept of lesbianism, inherited from sexology and Freudian discourses, and to redefine it in terms of a symbolic network of relationships between women. Interestingly, the novel introduces a range of female characters which may be seen as existing on a lesbian continuum from the two women in the sweetshop whom her mother forbids her to visit – 'She said they dealt in unnatural passions. I thought she meant they put chemicals in the sweets' (O, p. 7) – to Miss Jewsbury, who tells Jeanette that 'It's my problem too' (p. 106), and Jane, Doreen's daughter, who 'spends all her time at that Susan's doing her homework' (p. 76). Others such as Elsie Norris provide the practical support and non-judgemental friendship that Rich discusses. In an ironic turn, it emerges that Jeanette's mother had a close relationship with another woman whose picture Jeanette sees in a photo album dedicated to 'Old Flames' and whom her mother refers to as 'Eddy's sister' (p. 36). However, when Jeanette looks at the album again the picture has disappeared. In this case, Winterson records the erasure of lesbian existence documented by Rich.

As in the traditional genre, a dominant motif of the lesbian Bildungsroman is education, which is inextricably linked to the protagonist's discovery of love and sexuality. While in the majority of examples in the Bildungsroman tradition a younger woman is educated by a more powerful and (sexually) experienced older woman, in Oranges Jeanette's lovers are more like herself. Melanie works in the fish stall in the market and Katy is a convert to Jeanette's church. In fact Jeanette does have a sexual encounter with an older woman who happens to be a teacher, Miss Jewsbury, but does not experience it in positive terms; rather, 'We made love and I hated it and hated it, but would not stop' (p. 106). Jeanette's first sexual experience is represented as a private and 'innocent' affair, as yet unlabelled by the world as deviant or unnatural. Somewhat paradoxically, Jeanette is represented as simultaneously 'innocent' and fully sexual, thereby challenging the postlapserian view of sexuality. At first she feels no guilt about her sexuality and, in the context of a woman-centred culture, her actions feel perfectly natural. Winterson's emphasis on the naturalness of Jeanette's sexual feelings serves to represent lesbianism positively, in a manner at odds with the condemnatory discourse of 'Unnatural Passions' promulgated in the novel by the Church community. As Laura Doan states, Winterson's 'reconceptualization of the normal makes lesbian existence possible by, in effect, reversing the dominant culture's definition of natural and unnatural' and thus rendering 'heterosexuality as unintelligible' for many of her characters (1994, p. 138). If heterosexuality is represented as, by turns, asexual and perverse, lesbianism is the privileged site of sexual love.

In the second stage of her development, the Bildungsroman heroine's recognition of the fact that her love for women is atypical and her perception of it as socially illegitimate engender a confrontation with the outside world. In common with other post-1970s representations of lesbian identity, *Oranges* presents Jeanette's attitude as defiant rather than shameful despite the stigma the community attaches to her sexual orientation. It reacts punitively, by literally demonizing Jeanette. She is starved, beaten and forced to undergo a ritual exorcism of her 'demon'. Instead of incurring the more conventional psychiatric treatment of a 'sickness' undergone by other contemporary lesbian characters, Jeanette is punished as a sinner in the traditional religious manner. Owing to the emphasis placed on the mother–daughter relationship in the novel of development, it becomes particularly significant that it is the mother who betrays Jeanette by siding with the Church fathers against her. This is a pivotal moment in the text which explicitly aligns Jeanette's challenge to patriarchal and religious views of women's social and sexual role with feminism: 'The real problem it seemed was going against the teachings of St Paul, and allowing women power in the church', and that 'having taken on a man's world in other ways I had flouted God's law and tried to do it sexually' (pp. 133–134). As Jeanette bitterly comments, 'The Devil had attacked me at my weakest point: my inability to realise the limitations of my sex' (p. 134). But, whereas the intolerant religious community view Jeanette as a pariah, Winterson encourages readers to view her as a heroine. In an ingenious inversion of the demon motif, Jeanette accommodates her 'demon' and accepts her lesbian difference, saying that 'I'm not getting rid of you' (p. 109). It is possible to interpret Jeanette's 'demon' as a 'daemon', an aspect of herself which, in an internal dialogue, allows her both to express qualms about her lesbianism and to receive reassurance of its positive value. Winterson's use of elements of magical realism allows her to articulate the tension between 'victimhood' and 'heroism', and represents lesbian existence as a simultaneously dysphoric and euphoric experience.

As an example of postmodern metafiction, *Oranges* challenges 'narrative singularity and unity in the name of multiplicity and disparity' (Hutcheon, 1988, p. 90), and expresses what Brenda K. Marshall calls a 'postmodern awareness [. . .] that *both* history and literature are discourses', and thus not to be talked of in terms of truth, as much as "whose truth"' (Marshall, 1992, p. 150). The novel in fact begins with what has become a defining feature of Winterson's work: the deconstruction of 'grand narratives', especially History, rational philosophy and empirical science. In the manner of Lyotard (1984), she disputes the distinction between history as a series of objective facts and storytelling as a merely fictional account of the world. Rather, she insists that 'History should be a hammock for swinging and a game for playing' (O, p. 93), in which the primary activity is not one of 'unearthing' a pre-existing reality, but of creating or imagining the past. For Winterson, as for postmodern writers generally, history becomes another form of storytelling, with no more truth value but accorded more cultural status than 'fiction':

> Some people say there are true things to be found, some people say all kinds of things can be proved. I don't believe them. The only thing for certain is how complicated it all is, like string full of knots. It's all there but hard to find the beginning and impossible to fathom the end. The best you can do is admire the cat's cradle, and maybe knot it up a bit more.
>
> (p. 93)

Oranges argues for the validity of different, competing definitions of the real, endorsing discredited cosmologies and mythologies, and imbuing them with fresh explanatory power: folk tales, Greek myth, Grail legend, old wives tales are all seen as repositories for a human wisdom and way of knowing the world which is as truthful as orthodox, rational versions of reality. For this reason Winterson has been characterized as a purveyor of 'magic realism', a term coined to describe the strange mixture of realism and the fantastic that is encountered in the work of many contemporary writers such as Salman Rushdie, Angela Carter and Toni Morrison.

A major focus of the novel – indeed of Winterson's work as a whole – is the art of storytelling and its relation to public history and 'truth'. Jeanette is quintessentially a storyteller; she is both the narrator of 'her' story and a compulsive teller of tales. The narratives she purveys include the story of Daniel/Jonah in the lion's den/belly of the whale told in fuzzy felt, the narrative of salvation and accounts of saved souls in her church sermons, and the story of the Church camp in Colwyn Bay described in her school essay. The stories which Jeanette grows up reading and telling have one primary source – the master narrative of the Bible. For Jeanette's mother the biblical metanarrative explains the world, absolutely and unequivocally, and has application whether one is on a beach at Blackpool or in the jungles of Africa. In her early years the Bible holds the same explanatory power for Jeanette. But her gradual and painful recognition that the Bible is simply a story, an account of the world, that its truths are partial at best and lies at worst and that there are other stories which tell of different worlds and different ways of being provides the novel with its dramatic crisis, and signals her disillusion with metanarrative.

Winterson's use of fantasy serves to destabilize and interrogate the category 'auto/biography' by calling its truth into question, and by suggesting the existence of truths which autobiography, with its commitment to realism, cannot capture. At times, the faery sections of the novel serve to comment on the main narrative, and appear to stand as an analogue or parable of Jeanette's autobiographical tale. For instance, the tale of Winnet and the sorcerer parallels and illuminates, in the structure of its relationships and plot events, the story of Jeanette and her mother. Jeanette/Winnet is an adopted daughter whose mother/father wants her to keep alive the 'magic arts' and to 'take the message to other places' (p. 143). All goes well until Jeanette/Winnet's relationship with a 'stranger' displeases her mother/father, and leads to her expulsion from the community. Cast out, Jeanette/Winnet determines to travel to a great city where 'the city dwellers didn't sow or toil, they thought about the world' (p. 153). It is a place without betrayal, where truth matters, and the novel ends with Jeanette/Winnet on the threshold of this new world.

However, while the correspondences between the different narratives offer the reader the pleasures of recognition and re-reading the same tale across different genres, the different narratives are not reducible to each other. The myth sections do not paraphrase the action of the whole, nor do they merely supplement it by filling in the gaps in the language of fantasy. They serve to unsettle the seeming verisimilitude of autobiography through their uncanny presence in the larger narrative (a point missed by many mainstream commentators on the novel who largely ignored its mythic and postmodern elements). For what is at stake in the novel is the very incommensurability of different discourses; the understanding that they cannot be reduced to the same measure and that they literally speak of different worlds. As the author-narrator tells us in the novel's most self-referential section, 'Deuteronomy', 'I can put these accounts together and I will not have a seamless wonder but a sandwich laced with mustard of my own' (p. 95).

This discursive relativism or pluralism is articulated not only across the different narrative modes of the novel, but also within the autobiographical narrative itself. This occurs through the incursion of the fantastic and the supernatural into the 'real', so that the fantastic is seen to inhabit the discourse of the real, rather than simply being juxtaposed with it. For instance, the story of Winnet does not merely offer a mythical parallel to Jeanette's story; it inhabits it 'supernaturally'. Thus Winnet's lucky pebble appears in Jeanette's pocket. Similarly, the orange demon's possession of Jeanette makes no sense in terms of autobiographical realism or oral history. Nor can it be explained in the religious terms of devil possession employed by Pastor Finch. As the demon explains, rather than being the prerogative of the sinful, everyone is assigned a demon – 'the demon you get depends on the colour of your aura' (p. 108). Far from being emissaries from Satan, demons are 'just different'. Demonic possession does not entail a Manichean struggle in a world of absolutes, but an acceptance of difference, of being other-wise, and a commitment to different 'shades' of experience. That Jeanette accepts her demon signals her acknowledgment of her difference, of her 'orangeness' and of her lesbianism as a sign and expression of that difference. While *Oranges* represents lesbian identity as multiple rather than singular and unified, it is still posited as a more or less stable category: Jeanette's demon is after all an essential part of her. While the novel resists representing lesbianism as a revelation which resolves the protagonist's quest for identity, it is debatable whether it presents it purely as a fictional construct which is created in discourse. Certainly, the use of metafiction, polyphony and multiple narratives makes this a more open-ended text which encourages the reader to reflect on its construction rather than simply view its contents as a satisfying narrative of affirmation.

As Bonnie Zimmerman (1983, p. 245) points out, lesbian novels of development have historically offered three alternative resolutions: accommodation to, exile and escape from the patriarchal status quo.[2] Winterson's novel follows the trend of 1980s lesbian fiction to present a more qualified celebration of lesbian existence than was true of the fiction of the 1970s. One reason for this shift could be the changed political climate in Britain and North America, making utopianism a less viable fictional option. As Yvonne M. Klein comments, 'The expansive autobiographical lesbian novels of the seventies have something of a hollow ring when read in Thatcher's Britain or Bush's America' (1990, p. 330). Klein claims that novels such as *Oranges* and Audre Lorde's *Zami* from the same period 'occlude' their endings: rather than looking forward to a new lesbian community, they look back to childhood in order to 'reinvent a mythic history of female power' (1990, p. 70).

Thus, at the novel's end, Jeanette returns to her home town and has a reconciliation of sorts with her mother. The latter behaves as if Jeanette had never left home but arguably her very indifference suggests that Jeanette's difference has been accepted if not approved. Significantly, it is the mother who speaks the words of the novel's title when she philosophically admits that 'oranges are not the only fruit' (*O*, p. 172). Nonetheless, certain aspects of the resolution of *Oranges*, such as the depiction in symbolic terms of Oxford as the gateway to freedom for the lesbian artist, are defiantly utopian. Freedom – as an artist, as a lesbian, as a human subject – is not fully realized but remains a vision or dream of the future. As Bonnie Zimmerman comments of such fiction, lesbian community is envisaged as an imaginative space, just off the page (1983, p. 257).

Winterson's achievement in *Oranges* is thus to render lesbianism both normal and central to human experience. While this analysis has shown that she utilizes a discourse of difference to set Jeanette apart as 'one of the elect', nevertheless, the narrative as a whole, especially its identificatory processes, works to render her extraordinariness convincingly and emphatically ordinary. While this has proven to be Winterson's aim throughout her work, it is perhaps this first novel that comes closest to realizing it. Indeed, in her treatment of female relationships, Winterson may be seen to be answering Virginia Woolf's (1981) famous call for woman-centred texts in which 'heterosexual masculinity' is not the major term.

The most interesting feature of Winterson's contribution to the Bildungsroman genre is the way in which it simultaneously conforms to and exceeds generic boundaries and definitions. As Susana Onega comments, '*Oranges* is *both* linear and realistic *and* anti-linear and experimental' (2006, p. 19). On one hand, if it is read purely as a unique, literary work, it is raised out of the various generic, political and cultural contexts explored above. On the other hand, while conforming to many of the conventions of the lesbian genre, the text nevertheless exceeds them in aesthetic and ideological terms. Eschewing the term 'lesbian', the novel strives for a universal address. Rather than focussing on the marginal subject's difference, it brings the margins to the centre and makes difference the norm. And its stylistic diversity and experimentation set it apart from the rest of the lesbian genre. Although other works use myth (*Zami*) and comedy (*Rubyfruit Jungle*), very few include the range of discourses found in *Oranges* or combine them in such a self-consciously postmodern way. As Hilary Hinds observed,

> Having asserted its fluidity, its ability to cut across so many critical and cultural categories and positions, its refusal to be pigeon-holed as one sort of text or another, its appeal to a diversity of audiences, it is impossible to arrive at a conclusive statement about it. [But] any text that can transgress so many barriers deserves all the critical attention . . . it can get.
>
> (Hinds, 1992, p. 170)

ROMANCING HISTORY: *THE PASSION*

In her second major novel, Winterson moves beyond the autobiographical mode, adopting a form that Linda Hutcheon (1989) has termed 'historiographic metafiction', a mode of the postmodern novel which self-consciously explores the relationship between history and fiction, and questions what is meant by each. It foregrounds the role of storytelling and narrative in historical discourse and challenges the notion of history as a series of facts. According to Peter Brooker, this mode 'neither repudiates nor simply ironises the past; nor does it merely reproduce the past as nostalgia' (1992, p. 229). Instead,

> postmodernist fiction reveals the past [. . .] as always ideologically and discursively constructed. Its irony and use of paradox signal a critical distance within this world of representations, prompting questions not about 'the' truth, but 'whose' truth prevails. The political effect of this fiction therefore lies in the double action by which it inscribes and intervenes in a given discursive order.
>
> (Brooker, 1992, p. 229)

As in *Oranges*, the themes of love and personal integrity are uppermost, but juxtaposed with a narrative of lesbian love is the tale of a French soldier's hero-worship of Napoleon set during the Napoleonic wars of 1804–1815. The story is narrated in turn by each of the two protagonists, the male soldier Henri and the female Villanelle, a denizen of Venice caught up in Napoleon's conquest of Europe. The novel is therefore more ambitious in terms of both setting and narration than *Oranges*, but like her debut novel it similarly collapses the distinctions between then and now, fiction and the real, fantasy and fact. The 'passion' of the title is a polysemic sign, signifying simultaneously Henri's passion for Napoleon and then Villanelle; Villanelle's passion for the mysterious Queen of Spades; Napoleon's more banal 'passion' for chicken; and finally, by implication, the sublime 'passion' of Christ. As a work of historiographic metafiction, the novel privileges what Lyotard (1984) calls 'les petits récits', the little narratives that lie in the gaps of official recorded History. Rather than depict his advance across Europe from Napoleon's point of view, the novel presents the stories of the little people such as the infantrymen and the brothel whores caught up in the imperial project. Henri, for example, works in Napoleon's kitchen in the distinctly unheroic role of neck-wringer of Bonaparte's chickens. These alternative histories approximate to Michel Foucault's notion of 'counter-memory', defined by Brenda K. Marshall as follows:

> History, then, in Foucault's terms, may become 'counter-memory': the process of reading history against its grain, of taking an active role

in the interpretation of history rather than a passive, viewing role. Counter-memory *intervenes* in history rather than *chronicles* it.

(Marshall, 1992, p. 150)

Significantly, in an incorporation of autobiography, each narrator recounts their own story; Henri keeps a diary through-out the campaign and retrospectively writes his life as a memoir and Villanelle tells her story to Henri and the reader. Their narra-tives mirror each other, presenting the same events – Napoleon's advance across Europe, the occupation of Venice, the march on Moscow and the stories of their love affairs – from parallel per-spectives and setting the story of Henri's loss of heart for war and fighting against Villanelle's loss of heart to the Queen of Spades. Some readings regard these perspectives as conventionally gendered with Henri presenting a masculine and largely ratio-nalistic story and Villanelle providing a feminine and magical tale of love and loss. Paulina Palmer, for example, argues that Villanelle's narrative defeats Henri's 'in a contest between mascu-line and feminine principles for mastery of the narrative' (1998, p. 105). But this is surely a simplification given that in crucial respects Winterson inverts the relation between sex and gender in the novel: Villanelle, by virtue of her webbed feet, is rendered 'phallic' while the relatively passive Henri is feminized in both his attitudes and his relationships. Ironically, Henri emerges from the war without having killed anyone, but then murders the cook at Villanelle's behest, an act which 'hurts his mind' (*P*, p. 147) and is perhaps implicated in his self-exile in the madhouse at the end of the novel. It is probably more accurate to say that both their dis-courses are, in different ways, 'queered', as is their relationship to compulsory heterosexuality. Henri's first love is his mother, fol-lowed by his love of the motherland and his hero-worshipping of Napoleon, which is superseded by his unrequited passion for Villanelle, who has a child by him but will not marry him.

As in all Winterson's works, the novel contains several refrains: Henri's oft-repeated phrase 'I'm telling you stories. Trust me' (*P*, pp. 5, 13, 40) alludes to the theme of storytelling and its role in mediating, indeed sustaining, human life as well as to the issue of authorial reliability. Villanelle's two refrains – 'In between fear and sex, passion is' (pp. 55, 60, 62) and 'You play, you win, you play, you lose. You play' (pp. 43, 66) – gesture towards the theme of love as emotional risk represented by the motif of gaming. Desire,

Winterson suggests, is inevitably connected to the fear of loss: 'We gamble with the hope of winning, but it's the thought of what we might lose that excites us' (p. 89). Henri tells stories in order to ward off a sense of loss – of self as well as the beloved. The loss of the beloved – his mother, Napoleon and finally Villanelle – is precisely the incitement to narrate and may explain his refusal to leave the tower at the end of the novel. As Jennifer Gustar states, 'Instead of making his escape, he tells the story of his life in order to preserve his love. Henri fails to overcome his loss – to do the work of mourning – and passes into the terrain of melancholia' (2007, p. 61).

Like *Oranges* the novel blends a realist narrative with moments of magical incursion. The use of magic in this text takes two main forms: magical objects and magical attributes. The former include the icicle containing a thread of gold which the dying Domino leaves for Henri. Months later, when Henri thinks he has lost the piece of thread, Villanelle retrieves the icicle from her bag, still miraculously in its un-melted form. Some characters, like Patrick, possess magical attributes: his miraculous eye can apparently see young women undressing two villages away. Patrick tells stories about his native Ireland in which goblins live under the hills. As Henri observes, 'He was always seeing things and it didn't matter how or what, it mattered that he saw and that he told us stories. Stories were all we had' (*P*, p. 107). His observation points to one of the central themes of the novel: in impossible conditions, where life barely sustains itself, people tell stories to survive. As throughout her work, storytelling here performs a crucial human function: that of compensating for the deficiencies of reality and of making life endurable.

The novel's most important magical attribute, however, belongs to Villanelle and the story of her webbed feet makes up the beginning of the second section of the novel. As a result of a pregnancy ritual practised by the wives of boatmen that goes wrong, Villanelle is born with the webbed feet that are properly the mark of a male: 'there never was a girl whose feet were webbed in the entire history of boatmen' (p. 51). They serve as a metaphor for hybridity, a break with gender convention and a mark of Villanelle's difference. Like Virginia Woolf's hero(ine) Orlando, she possesses both male and female physical features and loves both men and women. Her name, Villanelle, is not literal either; referring to a poetic form, she also wears it 'as a disguise'

(p. 54). Towards the end of the novel, Villanelle asks Henri to retrieve her heart from the house of the Queen of Spades, where it has been since the end of their affair. Henri reacts in a baffled manner to this seemingly irrational request:

> Was she mad? We had been talking figuratively. Her heart was in her body like mine. I tried to explain this to her, but she took my hand and put it against her chest.
>
> 'Feel for yourself.'
>
> [. . .]
>
> I could feel nothing.
>
> (*P*, pp. 115–116)

Yet he does as she asks and is astonished when on entering the chamber he hears a 'regular steady noise, like a heartbeat' issuing from jar: 'The jar was throbbing. I did not dare to unstopper it. I did not dare to check this valuable, fabulous thing . . . ' (p. 120). Moreover, after killing the cook, Henri witnesses Villanelle apparently walking on water dragging their boats across the surface of the canal. And it is in Venice, 'the city of madmen' (p. 112), in Henri's words, in which he himself apparently goes insane.

The novel's depiction of Venice as a carnival space resonates strongly with the Bakhtinian concept of masquerade. Bakhtin states, 'The mask is related to transition, metamorphosis, the violation of natural boundaries, to mockery and familiar nicknames. It contains the playful element of life' (1984, p. 40). Like Villanelle, Venice represents a playful excess, both literal and figurative: an excess of water, sexuality and meaning. Variously described as a 'mercurial city' (*P*, p. 49), 'a city of mazes' (p. 49) and 'a city of disguises' (p. 56), it is a place of continual transformation that confounds rational minds. In this shifting world of canals and casinos, Villanelle is most comfortable at night, which, like Venetians' lives, is 'uncertain and temporary' (p. 57):

> In this enchanted city all things seem possible. Time stops. Hearts beat. The laws of the real world are suspended. God sits in the rafters and makes fun of the Devil and the Devil pokes Our Lord with his tail.
>
> (*P*, p. 76)

According to Judith Seaboyer, Venice as an imaginative construct 'recalls the ancient myth of the labyrinth, a fluid space of transformation and danger that has traditionally stood for the psychic inward journey, and increasingly for textuality itself' (1997, p. 484). In the stories of Henri and Villanelle, the novel provides highly self-reflexive and moving versions of this ancient journey mythos.

In a development from *Oranges*, which worked to naturalize lesbianism and render heterosexuality by inversion unnatural, the novel presents human sexuality as a whole as existing on a continuum. From the soldier with a reputation for liking 'firm buttocks' (*P*, p. 6), to Villanelle's polymorphous bisexuality – 'I am pragmatic about love and have taken my pleasure with both men and women' (pp. 59–60) – it presents a range of kinds of love and lover without privileging any. Indeed, rather than representing lesbianism as a superior choice, Winterson suggests that all love by its very nature entails a sense of compromise and loss of self regardless of object choice. Henri's observation that 'perhaps all romance is like that: not a contract between equal parties but an explosion of dreams and desires that can find no outlet in everyday life' (p. 13) holds true for Villanelle's passion for the mysterious woman whom she meets at the Casino, the Queen of Spades. Despite their shared gender, the Queen of Spades is a married woman who ultimately would not jeopardize her security for Villanelle.

The treatment of Villanelle's sexuality differs significantly from that of Jeanette in *Oranges*, which utilizes the 'lesbian continuum' model. Here, Winterson adopts, or appears to anticipate, another model which became influential in the early 1990s when Judith Butler elaborated her concept of gender as a kind of drag:

> Drag constitutes the way in which genders are appropriated, theatricalised, worn and done; it implies that all gendering is a kind of impersonation and approximation. If this is true, it seems, there is no original or primary gender that drag imitates, but *gender is a kind of imitation for which there is no original*; in fact, it is a kind of imitation that produces the very notion of the original as an effect and consequence of the imitation itself.
>
> (2004, p. 127)

Examples of drag and cross-dressing abound in the Venice sections of the novel, foregrounding both the artifice of the carnival city and the performative nature of gender. As Villanelle explains, 'I dressed as a boy because that's what the visitors like to see. It was part of a game, trying to decide which sex was hidden behind tight breeches and extravagant face-paste' (P, p. 54). According to Maria Aròstegui, Villanelle is the 'masquerader *par excellence*', who is 'not on the side of identity but on that of performance' (1996, p. 272). Winterson uses masquerade as 'a set of parodic practices' (p. 266) which serve to disrupt and re-signify gender categories and undermine the notion of natural sexual difference. Indeed, at one point, Villanelle asks, 'And what was myself? Was this breeches and boots any less real than my garters?' (P, p. 66). In Butler's terms, Villanelle's performance foregrounds the process whereby any gender is assumed. Its subversive potential means she can move in and out of identities rather than being fixed and trapped by them. However, the procedure does carry risk as is shown by her adding a fake moustache to her costume for protection. Moreover, whereas *Oranges* presented a somewhat uni-dimensional, if highly entertaining, image of masculinity, in that her male figures fall into one of three groups – beasts, non-entities and fanatical clerics – Winterson undertakes a much more nuanced exploration of male identity in *Passion*. In particular, she explores the constitutive role of violence in the construction of male identity and the implications of Henri's rejection of this role: 'Will you kill people, Henri?' (p. 8). As Henri observes of his and France's devotion to Napoleon, 'All France will be recruited if necessary. Bonaparte will snatch up his country like a sponge and wring out every last drop. We are in love with him' (p. 8).

The relationship between men may be one of camaraderie, as witnessed in the warmth of the bond between Henri and Patrick, a defrocked Irish priest. But men can exhibit sudden and mystifying – to Henri – acts of violence, as evidenced by the passionate anger of the man who burns his house down, and the cook's aggression towards his prostitute. In the face of this, Henri instinctively turns to the world of women such as the denizens of the brothel who protect each other against male violence and have an easy intimacy and solidarity that Henri, Prufrock-like, envies. In one of the few readings to focus on Winterson's depiction of men, Philip Tew argues that she explores masculinity with subtlety and

power as the striving for and inevitable failure of the heroic attitude (Tew, 2007). Some critics have interpreted this (male) failure
as Winterson setting up femininity as the position of power in
the text instead (see Palmer, 1998), but it should be remembered
that for all her desirability and magical character, Villanelle, too,
is left heart-broken towards the end of the novel. Indeed, this is
a novel as much about loss as it is about love. It presents parallel
stories about the (inevitable) disillusion of love. In the course of
the novel Henri goes from worshipping Napoleon – 'I was waiting for Bonaparte' (*P*, p. 15) – to hating him, which is perhaps an
aspect of passion, to accepting his flaws: 'What is more humili-
ating than finding the object of your love unworthy?' (p. 147). To
some extent the novel suggests the beloved is a fiction, the idealized projection of the lover onto the other: 'I invented Bonaparte
as much as he invented himself' (p. 158), an idea which forms
the basis for Winterson's subsequent novel *Written on the Body*.
What characterizes all these experiences is the subject's relation
to what Freud (1957) calls 'mourning and melancholia': in order
to love (again), one must accept loss. As Shiffer states, the text
'works continually to express loss so total and profound that it
cannot be spoken; it resides below the surface, within the silences'
(2004, p. 35). What is 'the valuable, fabulous thing' (*P*, p. 150) that
Villanelle talks of, if not desire itself, precious, elusive and difficult
to articulate? Villanelle's consolation is that subjectivity like desire
is shifting. 'I content myself with this; that where I will be will not
be where I am' (p. 150).

The novel's feminism, therefore, resides not only in Villanelle's
'feminine' discourse with its narrative of female struggle against
patriarchal oppression and the depiction of lesbian love in carnival Venice, but also in Henri's critique of militarism, of the
exploitation of women in war and of his horror of male violence against women. While Henri's youthful desire is directed
towards Bonaparte, his identification is with the women in his
life. These include his mother, who wanted to be a nun and
escaped an arranged marriage; the women in the army brothels,
whose side he takes against their brutish clients; and, of course,
Villanelle, whom he continues to love despite her rejection of
him. Moreover, his narrative provides an insight into male admi-
ration and envy of the bonds between women: 'She would never
do that for me' (p. 15), he laments when he sees one prostitute

comforting another. And he admires women's fortitude: 'They go on', he states. 'Whatever we do or undo, they go on' (p. 15). On one level the novel presents sexual difference in the starkest of terms. In a seemingly fundamentalist statement that echoes the old gender opposition between doing and being, Henri intones, 'Soldiers and women. That's how the world is. Any other role is temporary. Any other role is a gesture' (p. 45). And yet, while this depressing view appears to define the world of the novel, in fact its protagonists consistently and repeatedly prove otherwise, challenging rigid gender binaries. Just as Henri's sensitivity renders him unsuitable for soldiering, Villanelle's sexuality and choice of profession set her beyond the pale of conventional femininity.

POSTMODERN SEXUALITIES: *SEXING THE CHERRY*

In many ways a companion novel to *The Passion*, and like it an example of 'historiographic metafiction', *Sexing the Cherry* combines its historical setting – the English Civil War and Interregnum – with a fantastic narrative containing inset fairy tales. Like *The Passion*, the novel contains two alternating narrators, one female and one male – the rumbustious Londoner, Dog-Woman, and her foundling son, Jordan, who grows up to spend his life at sea on a restless quest for love and meaning. Each narrative is advertised by the presence of a fruity symbol: a banana for the decidedly phallic Dog-Woman and a pineapple for the adventurer-explorer Jordan. In addition to the features of historiographic metafiction and magic realism, the novel also evinces numerous examples of the carnivalesque and the grotesque, which work to destabilize normative categories of gender and sexuality. As discussed in relation to *Oranges*, magic realism refers to the combination of realism and the fantastic found in many contemporary novels, which works to call into question rationalistic conceptions of reality and to foreground alternative ways of knowing. The magical features of the text reside in the larger-than-life figure of the Dog-Woman (discussed below) and in the inset fairy tales in Jordan's narrative, particularly the story of the 12 dancing princesses.

In the Grimm brothers' original tale, every night 12 princesses leave their locked room to dance with 12 princes. The King sets a test: any man who can discover where his daughters go every night can marry the princess of his choice. Finally, a young soldier with the aid of an invisible cloak discovers their secret and he wins the eldest princess's hand in marriage and becomes heir to the throne. In Winterson's subversive rewriting of this patriarchal tale, the princesses provide their own 'and they lived happily ever after' ending: 'we did, but not with our husbands' (*S*, p. 48). One princess falls in love with a mermaid and runs away to live in 'perfect and salty bliss' (p. 48), while another has her husband embalmed in an inversion of Browning's poem 'His Last Duchess'. The third adores her beautiful male prince but he loves another boy and she jealously kills them both. The husband of the fourth princess is an adulterer who comes to a disease-ridden end; and the fifth reworks the Rapunzel story. Winterson's treatment of this story represents a 'queering' of the master narrative, providing a camp inversion or twist at the end. In her version, the lover is a woman and the prince turns into a frog: 'My own husband? Oh well, the first time I kissed him he turned into a frog. There he is, just by your foot. His name's Anton' (p. 52). As well as offering a comic take on the original, Winterson highlights the violence that often underlies traditional fairy tales as when the spurned prince 'forced her to watch while he blinded her broken lover in a field of thorns' (p. 53). The sixth princess looks back longingly to her single days when she was 'free to fly' (p. 53). Another sister reveals that 'the man I married was a woman' (p. 54) and celebrates their lesbian love. The eighth sister poisons her obese husband who then grotesquely explodes. The ninth princess is kept chained like a bird of prey and eventually tears out her husband's liver. The tenth sister's husband does not love her and has an affair, so she leaves him. The eleventh sister's husband asks her to kill him and she obliges.

In different ways, these intertextual reworkings serve to challenge patriarchal master narratives; to defamiliarize the taken-for-granted ideology of fairy tales; to draw attention to their frequently oppressive messages to young women to obey patriarchal dictates; and to reveal gender as a cultural construction. The fact that the retellings seem so extreme underlines their original power and violence. As Jordan points out, the story of the twelfth princess is missing. It turns out that Fortunata, the youngest sister, flies away on her wedding day, 'like a bird from a snare' (p. 60). Flying is one of the dominant motifs in the novel and represents freedom from constraints. As Mary Russo has shown, such examples of aerialism in women's writing and art represent 'fantasies, dreams, and visions of liberation' (1994, p. 13). Winterson articulates a feminist fantasy of weightlessness, conflating two types of freedom: of the patriarchal laws of society and the physical laws of gravity, time and history. 'She was so light that she could climb down a rope, cut it and tie it again in mid-air without plunging to her death. The winds supported her' (S, p. 60). Fortunata is a free spirit whose whereabouts are unknown; she alone escapes the patriarchal closure of the fairy tale.

Another key strategy of subversion deployed by Winterson derives from the concept of the 'carnivalesque', which Bakhtin employs to refer to a popular, anarchic and comic form of folk discourse in which the everyday rules and order are inverted or suspended. Carnivalesque discourse is multivalent and heterogenous, foregrounding spectacle, the macabre, 'low' body parts, bawdy language and the grotesque. In *Rabelais and his World*, Bakhtin defines the grotesque as 'exaggeration, hyperbolism, excessiveness' (1984, p.303), as that which 'protrudes from the body, [and] all that seeks to go out beyond the body's confines' (p.316). Moreover, for Bakhtin the grotesque body is quintessentially a female body, suggested by the figures of pregnant hags which 'combine senile, decaying, and deformed flesh with the flesh of new life' (1984, p. 26). As Mary Russo (1994) points out, this construction of the monstrous feminine is highly problematic for feminist readers, yet the image of the unruly woman also offers opportunities for a transgressive feminist cultural politics.

Winterson's depiction of the Dog-Woman represents an exemplary representation of the grotesque, her very name suggesting a mongrelized or hybridized identity:

How hideous am I?

My nose is flat, my eyebrows are heavy. I have only a few teeth and those are a poor show, being black and broken. I had smallpox when I was a girl and the caves in my face are home enough for fleas.

(S, p. 24)

She continues with a hilarious account of a travelling circus in which members of the public are invited to try to outweigh an elephant. No one comes close until Dog-Woman takes the chair and the following spectacle ensues:

> I took a deep breath, filling my lungs with air, and threw myself at the seat with all my might. There was a roar from the crowd around me. I opened my eyes and looked towards Samson. He had vanished. His chair swung empty . . . I looked higher, following the gaze of the people. Far above us, far far away like a black star in a white sky, was Samson.
>
> (S, p. 25)

Dog-Woman therefore represents an excessive femaleness, which is the source of both her power and her power to disturb, but she also in fact comes to represent excess *tout court*, one of the key features of the grotesque, as its original meaning – *grotto-esque*, an excess of decoration – suggests. Moreover, as Rabelais' original *Gargantua* demonstrated, the purpose of giants is to hold a mirror up to human vice, greed and folly. This is exactly what Dog-Woman achieves *vis à vis* the hypocritical Puritans who view her as a monster but themselves behave in monstrous ways.

Another key feature of the grotesque is the 'devouring and devoured body' which 'swallows the world and is itself swallowed by the world' (Bakhtin, 1984, p.317). Eating and drinking function as the means whereby man can devour the world or a part thereof without himself being devoured. However, women's bodies occupy an ambiguous position in that they can devour through sexual engulfment the male body, thus rendering them grotesque from a male perspective. This aspect of the female grotesque is foregrounded in the text when Dog-Woman is asked to perform fellatio on a stranger in the street and misinterprets his request: '"Put it in your mouth", he said. "Yes, as you would a delicious thing to eat." I like to broaden my mind when I can and I did as he suggested, swallowing it up entirely and biting it off with a snap' (S, p. 41). In another of her understandably rare sexual encounters Dog-Woman swallows a man whole:

> I did mate with a man, but cannot say that I felt anything at all, though I had him jammed up to the hilt . . . he complained that he could not find the sides of my cunt and felt like a tadpole in a pot. He was an educated man and urged me to try and squeeze in my muscles . . . I took a great breath and squeezed with all my might and heard something like

a rush of air through a tunnel, and when I strained up on my elbows and looked down I saw I had pulled him in, balls and everything.

(p. 106)

What these examples demonstrate is that Winterson does not merely reproduce the female grotesque as the exemplar of abjection as it is for Bakhtin, but rather transforms it into an image of power. As Lucie Armitt argues, in her book, *Contemporary Women's Fiction and the Fantastic*, Dog-Woman represents a 'grotesque hybrid challenging the accepted parameters of "normal" womanhood while, in this case, simultaneously plying with the pejorative sexual connotations' of her name (2000, p. 18). Armitt challenges Lynne Pearce's rejection of Dog-Woman as a feminist heroine on the grounds that she is a conservative Royalist who habitually uses violence, to argue that 'Dogwoman [*sic*] is an early-modern urban guerrilla . . . [and] a carnivalesque, excessive, womanly hero' (p. 19):

Yes, Dogwoman fights for the King against the puritans, yes, she is outrageous, dangerous, volatile and excessive, but she is a woman fully aware of being a woman, taking men on at their own games and beating them to a pulp in the process.

(Armitt, 2000, p. 20)

The novel also contains numerous examples of the carnivalesque discourse known as 'bawdy', in which an obscene and humorous sexual discourse is foregrounded, and 'low' words are habitually used to describe 'low' parts of the body. Dog-Woman's response to seeing the first banana brought back from the New World is typical: 'It's either painted or infected . . . for there's none such a colour that I know' (p. 12).

The question of Dog-Woman's sexuality is an interesting one: putatively heterosexual, she resists normative categorization. According to the view put forward by the French radical feminist Monique Wittig, she is more properly designated as lesbian: 'Lesbian is the only concept I know of which is beyond the categories of sex (woman and man), because the designated subject (lesbian) is not a woman, either economically, or politically, or ideologically' (1992, p. 20). (The Dog-Woman's modern day radical feminist counterpart would appear to lend weight to this theory.) Alternatively, both Dog-Woman's and Jordan's sexual identities may be understood in terms of Butler's theory of gender as performance. Through them Winterson provides a critique of normative gender roles and 'compulsory heterosexuality'. Butler argues that sex (biological bodies), gender (cultural attributes) and sexuality (desire and orientation) are not causally linked, natural and innate categories but rather produced in and through discourse and 'performativity':

> If gender is drag, and if it is an imitation that regularly produces the ideal it attempts to approximate, then gender is a performance that *produces* the illusion of an inner sex or essence or psychic gender core; it produces on the skin, through the gesture, the move, the gait (that array of corporeal theatrics understood as gender presentation), the illusion of an inner depth, necessity or essence that is somehow magically, causally expressed.
>
> (2004, p. 134)

In different ways, the characters enact Butler's theory of drag as the process whereby any gender is assumed. While Dog-Woman represents a violent transgression of normative gender roles, Jordan represents a more subtle and thoughtful challenge to sexual difference. In particular, he finds relief from oppressive binaries in cross-dressing: 'I have met a number of people who, anxious to be free of the burdens of gender, have dressed themselves as women and women as men' (p. 31). Here in Jordan's more philosophical outlook, the motif of transvestism becomes not simply a comic feature of carnival but a strategy for freedom of thought and movement. In a revealing passage, he describes the experience of crossing over into that 'foreign country' of the other sex:

> In my petticoats I was a traveller in a foreign country . . . I watched women flirting with men, pleasing men, doing business with men, and then I watched them collapsing into laughter, sharing the joke, while the men, all unknowing, felt themselves master of the situation and went off to brag in bar-rooms and to preach from the pulpits the folly of the weaker sex.
>
> This conspiracy of women shocked me.
>
> (*S*, pp. 31–32)

And, in an echo of both Virginia Woolf's *Orlando* and her arguments in *A Room of One's Own* (1981), Jordan's transgender experience lead him to a theory of gendered language:

> I noticed that women have a private language. A language not dependent on the constructions of men but structured by signs and expressions, and that uses ordinary words as code-words meaning something other.
>
> (S, p. 31)

The novel therefore presents a multiplicity of sexual identities existing on a continuum, which serves to 'queer' heterosexual normativity. Moreover, it promotes a model of species reproduction that relies not on a naturalized concept of heterosexual coupling, but on the horticultural concept of 'grafting':

> Grafting is the means whereby a plant, perhaps tender or uncertain, is fused into a hardier member of its strain, and so the two take advantage of each other and produce a third kind, without seed or parent.
>
> (S, p. 78)

As Doan argues, Winterson's ingenious model serves to 'call certain conceptual underpinnings into question and thereby breakdown restrictive parameters of the unimaginable' (1994, p. 153).

Like *The Passion*, *Sexing the Cherry* works as an example of 'historical' fiction which both interrogates (what is meant by) and intervenes in history. Winterson's use of parallel time frames and multiple characters serves as a means not merely to relativize history, but to suggest alternative trajectories and feminist histories. She performs the role of historiographic metafictionist described by Brenda K. Marshall and 'refuses the possibility of looking to and writing about the past "as it really was". Rather s/he takes on an active role, and "does" the past, participates, questions, and interrogates' (1992, pp. 50–51). Each of the characters has a modern-day counterpart who, reading linearly, suggests what that character might have become given different historical circumstances. Hence, the Dog-Woman becomes the maligned eco-feminist making a protest about environmental pollution on the banks of the river, and Jordan becomes the modern schoolboy Nicholas Jordan, misunderstood by his best friend for whom he harbours a secret passion. Alternatively, in a fantasy reading of the novel, which the text encourages, each set of characters exists simultaneously in a parallel world as a fantasy projection of themselves: the eco-feminist, thwarted and mocked in her/our own time, becomes the larger-than-life Dog-Woman whom no man can suppress, and Nicholas Jordan, whose homoerotic impulses are repressed, lives out a fantasy of sexual mutability. The magical no-place of fiction makes possible such journeys in space and time.

4

WRITTEN ON THE BODY,
ART & LIES AND *GUT*
SYMMETRIES

A LOVER'S DISCOURSE: *WRITTEN ON THE BODY*

In Winterson's simultaneously lyrical and analytical novel *Written on the Body*, the nameless narrator suffers an existential angst which finds only temporary relief in love affairs. Winterson utilizes the device of a sexually indeterminate narrator in order to effect a radical deconstruction of the romance genre and to celebrate the beloved's body in all its physical beauty and abjection. The novel concerns the love affair between the narrator and the beautiful, but married, Louise. When the narrator discovers that Louise has leukaemia, she/he leaves Louise in the belief that Louise's cancer specialist husband will give her the chance of life. Heartbroken at the loss of the beloved, the narrator retreats to the country and immerses herself/himself in medical textbooks to learn everything about the disease that threatens the beloved's life. Out of this Winterson fashions an extraordinary language of the body, in which the beloved's body is explored, excavated, categorized, fetishized and made love to. As Ginette Carpenter observes, 'the idea that the body can be read and re-read, written and re-written is the central motif of *Written on the Body*' (2007, p. 71).

Critical attention has been focused on the device of the sexually indeterminate narrator and how this figure is interpreted (see Lindenmeyer, 1999). The novel contains numerous codes, clues and references that suggest either a female narrator (and therefore a lesbian relationship) or a male narrator (and therefore a heterosexual or gay male relationship). Evidence of the narrator's feminine subject positioning is plentiful: 'I shall call myself Alice' (*WB*, p. 10); 'I stared at [the phone] the way Lauren Bacall does in those films with Humphrey Bogart' (p. 41); 'I felt like the girl in the story of Rumpelstiltskin' (p. 44); 'Why did I feel like a convent virgin?' (p. 94). But then male signifiers are just as commonly used to describe the narrator as 'Christopher Robin' (p. 61); 'a street yob' (p. 94); 'playing the Lothario' (p. 20); reading *Playboy* magazine (p. 36); and 'play[ing] the sailor and run[ning] a wife in every port' (p. 40). In order to decode such clues the reader is forced to rely on what linguists call 'background knowledge' (Montgomery et al., 1992) about gendered behaviour patterns – what we believe men and women generally do. However, it has to be remembered that such generalizations represent *stereotypes* of gendered behaviour and are not intrinsically 'female' or 'male', merely culturally coded as 'feminine' and 'masculine'. It is perfectly possible for women to enjoy reading *Playboy* and for a man to read women's magazines, both of which the narrator does. Winterson's narrative strategy serves to defamiliarize gender norms, making us question what we assume to be natural and normal for each sex. Moreover, there are moments in the text that both defamiliarize and 'unfix' gender and sexuality (as a range of practices and discourses) and foreground the unreliable narrator. In one such episode, the narrator describes Louise's transformative effect on her/him:

> She kissed me and in her kiss lay the complexity of passion. Lover and child, virgin and roué. Had I ever been kissed before? I was shy as an unbroken colt. I had Mercutio's swagger. This was the woman I had made love with yesterday, her taste was fresh on my mouth, but would she stay? I quivered like a school girl.
>
> (*WB*, p. 82)

While the conventional romance describes a highly gendered world of fixed sexual roles, Winterson invokes an array of mixed referents which work to invert and confound such roles. As Heather Nunn states,

> The stable body, the discrete gender and a clearly defined sexuality have formed the reference points of identification in numerous narratives of love and loss. The force and challenge of Winterson's fiction is in its offering up of an erotic experience that contests the conventional fixity of identity [. . .] The normative ideal of heterosexual

desire requires the production of discrete oppositions between the feminine and masculine attributes of female and male subjects. *Written on the Body* troubles this binary divide and arguably proliferates it to the point where it no longer makes sense.

(1996, pp. 16, 20)

In another self-reflexive example, the narrator plays with the reader, inviting a comparison with *Anna Karenina*'s Count Vronsky, saying teasingly, 'but I don't believe in living out literature' (*WB*, p. 75). While the refusal to fix gender may be experienced by some readers as frustratingly unsettling, for others it represents an exhilarating loosening of the bonds of gender.

This point is further demonstrated through the narrator's recounting of relationships with a string of female lovers who are invariably introduced by the phrase 'I had a girlfriend once' (*WB*, p. 19): Bathsheba (p. 16); 'a Dutch girl called Inge' (p. 21); Jacqueline (p. 24); Catherine (p. 59); Judith (p. 75); and of course Louise (p. 28). She/he then recalls male lovers with the litany 'I had a boyfriend once' (p. 92); these include 'Crazy Frank' (p. 92); Carlo (p. 143); and Bruno (p. 152). The male lovers are arguably culturally coded as gay through markers such as S/M preferences, nipple rings, and butch and camp discourse. However, the narrator also describes her/his relation to Louise as 'like a pair of 50s homosexuals' (p. 73), thus problematizing the ascription of literal referents to subjects. Similarly, Winterson transforms a putative description of (hetero)sexuality by emphasizing sameness rather than difference: 'I thought difference was rated to be the largest part of sexual attraction but there are so many things that are the same' (p. 129). While this may suggest a form of lesbian 'twinning'[1] – 'To remember you it's my own body I touch' (pp. 129–130), Winterson also gestures here towards the similarities of all human bodies regardless of sex. As Antje Lindenmeyer avers, 'By constructing a contradictory, "virtual" narrator from diverse sexual identities, she disturbs the concept of a "natural" stable heterosexuality as much as that of an essentially stable lesbian identity' (1999, p. 59).

Winterson stages a number of episodes which explore the narrator's ambiguous relation to both gender positioning and gender politics, particularly the politics of feminism. In one comic episode in which the narrator is reluctantly dragooned into helping her/his radical feminist girlfriend carry out an attack on male phallocentrism by blowing up some urinals, the narrator appears to alternate between a feminine voice, 'Why do men like doing everything together?', and a more masculine subject position, 'Would you mind finishing off?' (*WB*, p. 22). However, by rendering the scene comic, it is not clear who is actually the butt of the joke. Is Winterson poking fun at men's preoccupation with their penises, or at radical feminists who target such phallocentrism? The subversive humour cuts both ways as the narrator's sexual ambiguity highlights. In another episode of sexual indeterminacy the text explores the narrator's reaction to a phallic papier-maché snake which her/his girlfriend, Amy, has placed in the letter-box 'at crotch level' (p. 41). The narrator deals with this predicament, in which ringing the bell 'means pushing my private parts right into the head of the snake' (p. 41), by holding a dialogue in which two (possibly gendered) aspects of self debate its meaning. Part of her (female?) sees it as a jokey rebuke, while another part (male?) sees it as a threat inducing castration anxiety. The text appears to resolve the reader's uncertainty when Amy states 'You've nothing to be frightened of' (p. 42) as she demonstrates the trap's effectiveness on a leek. In a third example, fearful of having caught a sexually transmitted disease, the narrator visits a 'clap clinic'. From the perspective of gender positioning, the description is intriguing:

> I looked at my fellow sufferers. Shifty Jack-the-lads, fat businessmen in suits cut to hide the bulge. A few women, tarts yes, and other women too. Women with eyes full of pain and fear. What was this place and why had nobody told them? 'Who gave it to you love?' I wanted to say to one middle-aged woman in a floral print. She kept staring at the posters about gonorrhea and then trying to concentrate on her copy of *Country Life*. 'Divorce him,' I wanted to say. 'You think this is the first time?' Her name was called and she disappeared into a bleak white room.
>
> (p. 46)

The narrative sympathy appears to lie almost exclusively with women – apart from one dismissive reference to 'tarts'. In contrast, the narrator adopts a critical attitude towards the male sufferers. While this does not necessarily imply a female observer, it does suggest a feminine or even feminist viewpoint, seeing men's sexual irresponsibility as the source of much sexually transmitted diseases.

Ultimately, of course, the very ambiguity and instability of the narrative voice render such interpretations subjective, a point underlined by Winterson's use of a traditional novelistic convention – the unreliable narrator: 'I can tell by now that you are wondering whether I can be trusted as a narrator' (p. 24). Her/his account is self-avowedly subjective, and her/his view of others biased, as she/he admits regarding her/his rival for Louise's affection: 'I can't be relied upon to describe Elgin properly' (p. 92). Such narratorial instability suggests that 'gender' and 'sexuality' are largely products of reading strategies, and as Lindenmeyer argues,

> By constructing a lover/narrator whose gender remains undeclared, Winterson manages to unsettle perceptions of gendered difference. The text produces different meanings depending on whether the narrator is read as a man or a woman, and sexuality requires a basic human sameness from which a host of differences emerge that may or may not be gendered.
>
> (1999, p. 48)

The novel undertakes a simultaneous critique *and* celebration of romantic love, deconstructing and reconstructing the tradition of romance writing in order to remake it both stylistically and ideologically. Stylistically, Winterson is concerned to reinvent the *language* of romance, jettisoning the tired clichés and formulaic plots of the mainstream romance industry. Ideologically, too, she seeks to challenge the dominant political discourse of normative if not compulsory heterosexuality. The romance is one of the oldest literary genres, going back to the troubadour songs and tales of the Middle Ages, which were concerned with courtly love between knights and aristocratic ladies, heroic deeds and ordeals, and fabulous events, usually in an idealized pastoral setting. In the eighteenth century the gothic romance emerged as a mode in which a female heroine replaced the medieval male quest figure, and was tested in a series of assaults on her moral and physical person, carried out by an aristocratic rake who sought to seduce her. Developing as a popular, sometimes supernatural, counterpoint to literary realism in the nineteenth century, the romance developed into a mass market industry in the twentieth century, fuelled by fantasies of true love rather than the fantasy creatures and events of the medieval genre.

The novel contains references to all these varieties of the romance. For example, the narrator is repeatedly figured as a heroic quester in the tradition of the medieval romance genre. In the central section of the novel detailing the cancer attack on Louise's body, the narrator represents himself as the knight protecting his Lady, 'will you let me stand guard over you, trap them as they come at you?' (*WB*, p. 115); and as the Lover-adventurer, 'Explore me', you said and I collected my ropes, flasks and maps' (p. 119). Louise is 'a Pre-Raphaelite heroine' (p. 99), drawn from nineteenth-century Romantic art and reminiscent of a 'heroine from a Gothic novel, mistress of her house, yet capable of setting fire to it and fleeing in the night with one bag' (p. 49). Her beauty, glamour and exoticism set her apart from the modern day and render her a highly romantic and other-worldly figure of fantasy. There are also numerous references to the modern day romance industry, which in contrast to the traditional allusions are invariably negative. Indeed the narrator is scornful of the clichés and debased character of contemporary romance, particularly the culture of domestic heterosexuality, with its sentimental greeting cards and bridal magazines. Viewing romance as a substitute for real passion, she/he comments that most of us settle for 'the diluted version, the sloppy language, the insignificant gestures. The saggy armchair of cliches' (p. 10). Indeed, 'It's the clichés that cause the trouble' (pp. 10, 21, 26, 71, 155, 180) stands as the novel's refrain. The narrator expounds a scathing critique of postmodern relationship culture including computer dating, virtual sex and what Winterson calls 'teledildonics' (p. 97). Against this, she asserts an older model of romance, privileging material over virtual reality – 'For myself, as unreconstructed as I am, I'd rather hold you in my arms' (p. 97) – in a statement that prefigures the theme of her 2000 novel, *The PowerBook*.

The novel also draws on the contrasting mode of anti-romance which, as its name suggests, works to invert and thereby challenge the traditional conventions of the romance. Whereas romance speaks in a heightened, poetic language, the anti-romance is a cynical, disillusioned mode which uses a more realist paradigm of everyday commonplace language to reveal the gap between (sexual) fantasy and reality. While romance emphasizes sexual love as a transcendent, quasi-spiritual experience, which unites the lovers, the anti-romance adopts a demythologizing approach and undermines the myths of merger and sexual transcendence. While the heroines of romance fiction find themselves through the love of good (wo)man, the anti-heroes of anti-romance are essentially alienated and alone. This is underlined by the first-person narration of *Written*, which foregrounds a highly subjective, individualistic and narcissistic self. The novel addresses the painful and lonely aspects of human desire and identity, representing an experience of dislocation rather than integration, frequently working against the grain of feminist discourse and its tenet of woman-identification.

In the anti-romance mode the protagonist is portrayed as openly sizing women up; the gaze is represented as overtly sexual and consuming, thereby breaking the feminist injunction against the objectification of women. Repeatedly throughout the novel the narrator objectifies Louise in a way reminiscent of the male gaze. For the narrator who falls in love with her and for the reader who only glimpses her through the narrator's mediating gaze, she is frequently presented as a sight:

> ... Louise strode through the door, her hair piled on her head and pinned with a tortoiseshell bar. I could smell the steam on her from the bath and the scent of a rough woody soap. She held out her arms, her face softening with love, I took her two hands to my mouth and kissed each so slowly so that I could memorise the shape of her knuckles.
>
> (WB, pp. 50–51)

Notwithstanding the obvious *energy* Louise displays here, for Lucie Armitt (2007) *Written* marks the moment when Winterson abandons a specifically female *voice* in favour of depicting the woman's *body*. 'I realised how often other people looked at Louise' (WB, p. 31), the narrator tells us, and this increases her desirability for the narrator, making her a beautiful covetable object. At times such as this, the narrator is oblivious to her/his objectification of the beloved. At other times, however, she/he is acutely and ironically aware of her own complicity in romantic and patriarchal ideologies. On being accused by Gail of running out on Louise, the narrator thinks, 'That doesn't sound like the heroics I had in mind. Hadn't I sacrificed myself for her? Offered my life for her life?'

(p. 159), and in an explicit reference to the courtly love tradition asks, ' "Who do I think I am?" Sir Launcelot?' (p. 159). Arguably, then, the text deconstructs the very strategies of romantic objectification that inform the narrator's discourse.

As Carpenter points out, the novel acknowledges that 'the conventional language of romance is an inadequate tool for capturing the complexities of love and desire' and pivots on the paradox that 'this love that is purportedly beyond language has to be written and read in the very language that it claims to be beyond' (2007, p. 73). Trying to find ways of expressing her/his love to Louise, the narrator worries that the phrase 'I love you' has been emptied of meaning: 'The more I underlined it the hollower it sounded' (*WB*, p. 52). One of the key ways Winterson challenges romantic cliché is through the use of estranging scientific and medical discourses of the body in the central section of the novel. For example, a romantic description of Louise's face is preceded by a distinctly factual definition:

THE FACE: THERE ARE THIRTEEN BONES THAT FORM THE SKELETON OF THE FACE. FOR COMPLETENESS THE FRONTAL BONE SHOULD BE ADDED.

Of the visions that come to me waking and sleeping the most insistent is your face. You face, mirror-smooth and mirror-clear. Your face under the moon, slivered with cool reflection, your face in its mystery, revealing me.

(*WB*, p. 132)

By mixing together contrasting and apparently antithetical registers of scientific and romantic discourse – the language of anatomy and the language of feeling – the text works to defamiliarize our understanding of the sexual body with the result that we see beyond the clichés and conventions of each discourse whether medical or erotic. Moreover, Winterson forges a reinvigorated language of love out of the hybridized discourses, capable of crossing the boundaries of both gender and genre. In another entry on the skin, the narrator muses, 'Odd to think that the piece of you I know best is already dead' (p. 123). The novel explores the paradox that the external body can be beautiful and perfect, while the inner body is diseased and killing itself and thereby challenges the privileging of the surface of the body characteristic of the romance mode. Moreover, the narrator refuses to see the lover's (diseased) body as abject or grotesque: 'There is nothing distasteful about you to me' (p. 124). Indeed, every anatomical part – blood, bone, cells, tissues, cavities, muscle, cartilage – becomes precious to the narrator as a part of Louise: 'Within the clinical language, through the dispassionate view of the sucking, sweating, greedy, defecating self, I found a love-poem to Louise' (p. 111). The text therefore renders the grotesque sublime and translates the abject into poetry, and as Carpenter observes, 'Linguistic slippage between the discourses of the body, desire and disease is celebrated as perhaps the one space where love can find expression' (2007, p. 73).

This resignifying of the grotesque does not extend throughout the text, however. Significantly, the lovers the narrator rejects – Jacqueline and Gail – are not beautiful romantic heroines, but ordinary-looking women who clearly cannot compete with Louise. Jacqueline is represented as a rather pitiful and abject figure with 'her beret pulled against the drizzle' and holding 'a carrier bag full of food, leeks prodding through the sides' (WB, p. 55). Gail is represented in terms of the grotesque, and unflattering descriptions of her appearance abound: 'She had a vast bottom' and 'exhausted make-up' (p. 143). Her body sags, she snores heavily, and she smells of 'dry rot' (p. 144). Recalling the monstrous size of Dog-Woman, Gail is described as 'a three-ton truck on a slope' (p. 159). After a sleepover at the narrator's cottage, Gail 'looked like a prime cut of streaky bacon. Her eyes were small and red from the night before. Her hair stuck out like a straw rick. I shuddered' (p. 147). Most damning of all, watching Gail devour a greasy bacon sandwich makes the narrator sick – 'I got to the toilet just ahead of my vomit' (p. 148). Vomiting and shuddering are both characteristic responses to abjection and represent extreme attempts to expel the abject image or part. The strength of her/his revulsion surprises even the narrator: 'Why are you so horror-struck by a woman whose only fault is to like you?' (p. 147). But despite the narrator's shame-faced acknowledgement, in this respect the text fails to dispel the privileging of Louise's beautiful if sick body over Gail's healthy but unattractive one. The idea of the beautiful dying woman is of course a central part of the Romantic imagination (see Bronfen, 1992). Art, literature and opera abound with images of consumptive heroines whose illness renders them even more desirable. As the narrator comments,

'She would be very thin, my beautiful girl, thin and weary and lost' (p. 102).

Nevertheless, as the critic Lynne Pearce argues, Winterson presents a thoroughly writerly, in the Barthesian[2] sense, account of love and desire, viewing them as continually in the process of being scripted and rescripted: 'Winterson's novels belong to a long, intertextual tradition of literature that has been inscribed by, and is itself reproductive of, this most seductive and resilient of discourses' (1993, p. 163). The metafictional aspects of Winterson's work therefore become crucial: 'Since romantic love exists as a narrative discourse, learnt by us "as story", our salvation lies in our ability to re-write it' (Pearce, 1993, p. 164). Pearce highlights how Winterson's work deconstructs the official 'Lover's Discourse' through humour, parody and subversion. 'Winterson's rewriting of romantic love depends crucially on an awareness of both sexual difference and a disruption/inversion of narrative conventions' (*ibid.*, p. 156). And she argues that 'Winterson's success in providing alternative models of lesbian romantic love has gone hand in hand with her adoption of an anti-realist mode of story-telling' (*ibid.*, p. 165).

As well as being highly metafictional and intertextual, foregrounding the *genre* of romance writing and interrogating its politics, rather than simply telling a love story, the novel's discourse on sexual difference, the way it represents femininity and masculinity, approximates to Cixous's concept of 'écriture féminine', or feminine writing. Winterson's narrator's mutual 'reading' of Louise's body, her celebration of it in heightened, poetic language, the representation of identity and subjectivity as fluid and shifting and, most importantly, the metaphor of the body as a text, all approximate to écriture féminine:

> Who taught you to write in blood on my back? Who taught you to use your hands as branding irons? You have scored your name into my shoulders, referenced me with your mark ... Written on the body is a secret code only visible in certain lights; the accumulations of a lifetime gather there ... I didn't know that Louise would have reading hands. She has translated me into her own book.
>
> (*WB*, p. 89)

Interestingly, Winterson's text makes explicit intertextual allusion to another French feminist work, Monique Wittig's *The Lesbian*

Body (1975). In Wittig's original text, the slash operates to exemplify the radical splitting of the subject:

> M/y most delectable one I set about eating you, m/y tongue moistens the helix of your ear delicately gliding around, m/y tongue inserts itself in the auricle, it touches the anti-helix, m/y teeth seek the lobe, they begin to gnaw at it, m/y tongue gets into your ear canal.
>
> (1975, p. 24)

Wittig, unlike Winterson, makes clear the relation of her discursive strategy to lesbian poetics, naming the body as 'lesbian': 'THE LESBIAN BODY THE JUICE THE SALIVA THE SPITTLE THE SNOT THE SWEAT THE TEARS' (1975, p. 28). Nevertheless, Winterson's text mimics Wittig's in its lists of body parts and radical alternative taxonomy of the (female) body. The narrator's reading/lovemaking works to deconstruct – quite literally – the body as a stable, gendered entity. As Nunn states,

> The litany of all the bodily parts and the dismemberment of the body underscore the traditional fragmentation of the woman's body. The lover literally rips and tears her lover apart, challenging the fetishization of the female body by worshipping all of its elements: the tissues, the scar, the anus, the filthy bloodstream, the womb, the gut, the brain, the skin cells, the skeletal bones . . . '
>
> (1996, p. 25)

The novel also appears to question the essentialist model that arguably underlies theories of écriture féminine, deconstructing the binary model that posits femininity against masculinity. It would therefore be incorrect to read *Written* purely as an example of a specifically feminine writing practice. It could be argued that it is the very destabilizing of gender and sexual difference that characterizes the postmodern lesbian aesthetic used by Winterson. As Nunn argues, the lesbian 'transgresses the masculine/feminine binarism and opens up a space for a fluidity of movement across identifications' (1996, p. 21) In this respect, Winterson's narrative practice in *Written* approximates best to what Eve Kosofsky Sedgwick (1994) delineates as a 'queer' mode of signification full of gaps, and excesses of meaning. The ending of the novel is suitably and characteristically occluded: on the level of 'story', the reader is left wondering whether Louise really has returned to the lover or whether the lover merely dreams she does.

A HYMN TO THE BOOK: *ART & LIES*

Art & Lies: A piece for three voices and a bawd is Winterson's most experimental work, and the most controversial, garnering more critical reviews than any of her other books. It is also arguably her most melancholic work; its sombre tone contrasts greatly with the exuberance of *Oranges* published nearly ten years previously. As the Biographical Reading attests, the novel was written at a difficult stage of Winterson's life and career and this appears to carry over into the work. A highly literary novel about aesthetics and the function of art, which it identifies as a means 'to escape the arbitrary nature of existence' (*AL*, p. 186), it is also amongst her most polemical works, exploring both the injustices of history, particularly for women, and the malaise of contemporary life. Set simultaneously and disconcertingly in 600 BC and 2000 AD and subtitled *A piece for three voices and a bawd*, the novel eschews realist historical setting altogether, occupying an autonomous realm much as a piece of music does. The voices of the title belong to three 'characters' which are clearly named for historical figures: Handel the composer, Picasso the painter and Sappho the poet. Handel is a surgeon specializing in breast cancer and erstwhile Catholic priest; Picasso, whose real name is Sophia Montgolfier, is a young female painter who has suffered abuse at the hands of her family; and Sappho is the Greek poet of sixth-century Lesbos. Their different stories are juxtaposed in a fragmented, disorienting narrative, which nevertheless comes together when it emerges that they are all travelling on a train heading for the Aegean coast. However, as Winterson attests, the protagonists 'are not characters in the physical sense that we know them on the street or perhaps even in our own lives. They are consciousnesses' (Wachel, 1997, p. 67). Indeed, this is a journey of the imagination, through fictional worlds and textual spaces.

The 'bawd' of the title refers to Doll Sneerpiece, who appears as the author of an eighteenth-century memoir and piece of literary pornography along the lines of John Cleland's *Memoirs of a Woman of Pleasure* and allows Winterson to pursue in humorous, parodic fashion the analogy between writing/reading and sex that characterizes all her work. In addition to Doll's memoir, the novel contains other examples of invented and inventive texts, from Latin pastiche to Sapphic verse. Winterson utilizes the conceit of a book within a book to demonstrate the intertextual relationship between her 'characters' and, by extension, her readers. At the beginning of the novel Handel tells us, 'I was not the first one to find the book' (AL, p. 3), suggesting its passage through time and many hands; and 'this book had not been finished, unfinished by whom? The reader or writer?' (p. 3), which alerts the reader to another, metafictional level of the text. Later, the narrator tells us, 'The Book was his but not his' (p. 202). When Handel falls asleep on the train it is picked up first by Picasso and then by Sappho, who continue to read Doll's adventures. And just as Sappho reads Doll's story, Doll in turn reads Sappho's poems in a mutual, *mise en abyme* exercise of each reading the other. It also appears that the memoir is part of a portfolio of works by Bede, Boccaccio and Goethe among others, as well as classical works by Homer and Ovid from the Great Library at Alexandria. The 'book' thus refers not simply to one single text but, intertextually, to the whole canon of Western Literature. The novel ends not with the word 'Fin', but with an extract from Strauss's light opera *Der Rosenkavalier* followed by a series of blank pages, presumably suggesting the reader may well complete the book in their own way.

The novel presents in exemplary fashion Winterson's philosophical vision at this time, encompassing an uncompromising anti-realist aesthetic which insists that 'language is artifice' (p. 184) and 'art is not supposed to be natural' (p. 185), and a rejection of the opposition between material and non-material realms which states that 'Materialists and spiritualists alike seem to me to have missed the point; as long as we are human we are both' (p. 118). In common with *Art Objects*, the collection of essays written at the same time, Winterson puts forward the aesthetic credo that art is timeless and self-sufficient: 'All art belongs to the same period' and 'Art defeats time' (p. 67). The novel sees art as one of the only defences against philistinism and launches a diatribe against the emotional deadness of contemporary culture. In particular, the novel is concerned about the moribundity of language and, echoing the modernist views of T.S. Eliot and Samuel Beckett, it expresses a fear that language is exhausted: 'Delicate words exhausted through over-use' (p. 65). Extending the project she began in *Written*, Winterson seeks to re-energize literary language through the devices of estrangement, register mixing and metaphorical substitution. As in that novel her central metaphor is writing/speaking as a sexual act: 'The word and the kiss are one. Is language sex? Say my name and you say sex' (p. 66). Her aim, to paraphrase Shklovsky's (1965) dictum about the function of art ('to make the stone stony') is to make sex sexy again by deforming the language of sexual love. She eschews typically romantic words and phrases for striking, iconoclastic and sometimes obscene language such as in the extraordinary image of language as a strap-on dildo:

> This is the nature of our sex: She takes a word, straps it on, penetrates me hard. The word inside me, I become it. The word slots my belly, my belly swells the word. New meanings expand from my thighs. Together we have sacked the dictionary for a lexigraphic fuck.
>
> (*AL*, p. 74)

In an exuberant rewriting of eighteenth-century literary pornography, Winterson foregrounds the desire and the agency of the woman in her pursuit of sexual satisfaction and shows a similar historical interest in sexual minority cultures that she demonstrated with Villanelle in *The Passion*. Like Cleland's heroine Fanny Hill, Doll Sneerpiece breathlessly records in minute physiological detail the many and various sexual peccadillos of the men and women she encounters. Doll desires a young man called Ruggiero, who rejects her advances making her suspect he is a homosexual – 'surely he is not a gentleman of the backdoor?' (*AL*, p. 79). Her narrative is full of such bawdy jokes and obscene puns, referencing 'low' or sexual parts in carnivalesque fashion. When Doll, in an effort to win Ruggiero's heart, cross-dresses and becomes 'a breeches Doll' (p. 80) and pursues him to a tavern, we are introduced to what historians such as Alan Bray and Randolph Trumbach have identified as 'sodomitical subcultures' (Trumbach, 1987), which emerged in London in the early eighteenth century. Bray (1995) emphasizes the historical significance of the 'mollies', effeminate men who desired other men, as early forerunners of the modern homosexual, often in the so-called 'molly houses', taverns in which queer subjects could cross-dress and 'mimick all manner of Effeminacy' according to one contemporary source (Ward, 1756, p. 9). The scene is treated comically in the manner of Restoration comedy or a picaresque novel, and ends with Doll, dressed as a man, seducing Ruggiero, dressed as a woman, by reading to him from Sappho's poems. A later, indeed climactic, instalment of the seduction sees Doll at the point of penetrating Ruggiero with her porcelain dildo. Newton, the great Enlightenment mathematician is on hand to offer advice on how to extract the dildo. In a hilarious parody of Newton's *Principia Mathematica*, Doll asks Newton to 'calculate the force required to remove this lewd pin from those innocent buttocks' (*AL*, p. 167), which, after applying the formula $\pi r2\, l \times p$, culminates in a spectacular, grotesque 'volley of farts' (p. 168) that sends Ruggiero soaring off the bed.

As in *Written on the Body*, '[r]eading and desire, or, more specifically, sexual desire, become metaphors for each other; the relationship between reader and text is as intimate, as visceral, as that between lovers' (Carpenter, 2007, pp. 74–75). As Carpenter points out, Doll's tale and her bawdiness throw into relief Handel's asceticism and Picasso's pain. Doll reads life far more fluently than either Handel or Picasso and her skill is reflected in the dextrous way she is able to combine prostitution and self-education:

> She had found that by arching her bottom in a calculating manner, she could prop her forearms on the bed and continue to read undisturbed by the assaults on her hypotenuse. It was in this way that she had come to delight in the elevating works of Sappho.
>
> (*AL*, p. 29)

Apparently drawing a comparison between the eighteenth century's lack of sexual restraint and the late-twentieth-century excess, Winterson juxtaposes Doll's narrative with that of Handel, an ascetic figure who advocates self-restraint on the grounds that freedom of choice has led not to satisfaction but to lack of feeling. Describing himself thus, 'I, Handel, doctor, Catholic, admirer of women, lover of music, virgin, thinker, fool' (p. 26), Handel is about to leave the city 'never to return' (p. 26). In many ways he represents an older version of the earlier Wintersonian males, Henri and Jordan, including their critical views of social and sexual roles. Moreover, it emerges that Handel is a castrato, given the illegal operation before puberty on the word of his elderly mentor and lover, a Catholic cardinal.

Through the voice of her male narrator, Winterson undertakes a sustained and sometimes angry denunciation of Western culture, calling it 'a modern wretchedness new to history' (p. 146). In an angry protest reminiscent of Winterson's *Times* columns, the narrator indicts a range of modern ills from EU regulation to Heritage Britain, in particular lambasting the domestication and 'touristification' of the countryside: 'My advice is to stick to the paths, which lead in a Dantesque descent, from the car parks to the toilets, to the gift shops, to the Heritage Museum' (p. 104). Handel expounds an anti-capitalist view, rejecting the various 'gods of money, gods of fame . . . all the brazen gods of the material world' (p. 145) and articulates a critique of progress that chimes both with the anti-globalization and green movements of the 1990s and 2000s and with the postmodern critique of the Enlightenment metanarrative of progress:

> For progress read 'technology'. The same old material world, this time in a space suit made of DNA. How To Fight Time the Techno Way. Heart transplant. New mistress. New car. Bigger Better Bomb. Tag and kill the ageing gene. Face lift for now. Nintendo for the kids. Virtual Reality for the grown-ups. Eat more irradiated food. Feeling ill? Radiotherapy, chemotherapy, bowel out, breasts off, we have a robot to take care of you . . . Fear of death? Get in the freezer. We'll thaw you out when we can . . . The kingdom of heaven is within you.
>
> (pp. 146–147)

Handel rejects the selfish materialism and individualism of Western culture, at one point interweaving platitudes of everyday discourse with the unspoken subtext 'how shall I live?' (p. 25). As a doctor and cancer surgeon Handel has been responsible for carrying out mastectomies. Disapproving of the callousness of colleagues in the profession who treat women's bodies as meat, he empathizes with the women in his care and tries to set them at ease. He is haunted by medical errors and decisions taken in the past: once when as a Catholic he refused a woman an abortion; and again when following a mix-up he cut off the wrong breast of a cancer patient. As Carpenter comments, 'The grand narratives of science and religion are exposed, through Handel, as purveyors of lies, their jargons and practices disguising their deceptions' (2007, p. 75). Another case furnishes an extraordinary story which is narrated twice (*AL*, pp. 18, 182) with the wry admission 'There is more to the story than I told you at the time' (p. 178) and which, it transpires, connects all three narratives: Handel was the doctor who attended Picasso's mother during labour, and aided the birth by performing cunnilingus on her.

In the Picasso sections, the novel develops a familiar Wintersonian theme, expressed in *Written* and elsewhere, that marriage is inimical to passion. Calling newly-weds, 'newly-deads' (*AL*, p. 160), it asks, 'What was desire? Certainly not the safe excursions into family life' (p. 82). The text echoes Henri's mother in *The Passion*: 'It is better to burn than to marry' (*P*, p. 9) and extends the critique of the nuclear family that Winterson had begun in a lighter vein in *Oranges*. Here, in contrast, the family is presented as violent and destructive. Lambasting 'the sick semantics of family life' (*AL*, p. 82), Winterson's depiction accords with the critique of second wave feminism that far from nurturing and supporting its female members the family can operate as the site of oppression and abuse. Picasso's brother rapes and abuses her throughout her childhood and her parents turn a blind eye; while he goes off to Sandhurst, she attempts suicide and is admitted to psychiatric hospital. After recovery and a confrontation with her family, her father tries to have her re-committed and finally attempts to murder her rather than let the truth of the abuse come out. Winterson depicts the psychological toll this takes on Picasso's young mind: 'She had learned to hate her body because he said he loved it' (p. 82). Switching between first- and third-person narration, Picasso's story exemplifies both the injustices meted out historically to creative women and a testimony to women's survival. It registers the need for women to take control of their lives: 'I picked up my paint brush and began' (p. 45). In a restaging of Sappho's death from the cliff-top on Lesbos, Picasso's suicide is presented as a female version of the Icarus myth:

> She made wings out of feathers she found [. . .] Her opening aileron makes a pause in the too smooth current that bears her down. For a moment she can hover *à la belle étoile*. She told me her name was Montgolfier but she spelt it ICARUS.
>
> (p. 73)

In both scenes, just as in previous novels, Winterson draws on the metaphorical associations between flight and freedom to create a liberating mythos for her female characters.

The Sappho sections are among the most interesting in the novel in that through them Winterson explicitly addresses an issue which exists as a subtext in many of her works: the historical erasure of lesbian existence. Exploring the construction of Sappho the poet by the male literary establishment, she points out both the critical obsession with her as a sexual icon – 'say my name and you say sex' (p. 51) – and the relative lack of scholarly editions of her work: 'Her name has passed into history. Her work has not' (p. 69). The first-person lament, 'My own words have been lost against theirs' (p. 52), perhaps echoes Winterson's sense of her own treatment by the media at this point in her career. She charts the way in which Sappho has been inserted into a patriarchal narrative of 'compulsory heterosexuality' (Rich, 1993), beginning with the poet Ovid: 'The poet Sappho, for love of Phaeon the ferry man, who spurned her, flung herself from the cliffs of Lesbos, into the dark Aegean sea' (*AL*, p. 72). In contrast to this stereotypically feminine ending, Sappho's death falling from a cliff is rewritten by Winterson as a glorious act of self-assertion: the 'breaking voice in an ecstacy of praise' (p. 75). A child of Hermes and Aphrodite (hence Hermaphrodite), Sappho is another of Winterson's compelling bisexual creations. She is also, of course, a lesbian; indeed, Winterson uses the term, pointedly and ironically, as a literal signifier of origin as well as of sexuality: 'Sappho (Lesbian *c*. 600 BC Occupation: Poet)' (p. 72). Rejecting the heterosexual inscription of Sappho, Winterson's text resituates Sappho in a distinctively lesbian context, presenting her work as inspired by the love of women: 'Not for love of you Phaeon but for loss of her' (p. 72). In a wonderful example of écriture féminine Sappho makes a lyrical address to her lover:

> Love me Sophia, in my foolishness, love my words and not my mortal remains. Be tidal to me in the constancy of change. Break over me where I feel most safe, be a shore to me, when I fear I am wave in the water, endlessly slipping away. Lift me up like a shell from the beach, now empty, now full. Lift me up and there are still songs.
>
> (p. 57)

While Handel and Picasso's accounts alternate between first- and third-person narratives, Sappho's narrative is written largely in the second person, addressing the other woman as 'you' in a way reminiscent of Luce Irigaray's 'When our lips speak together':

> I love you: our two lips cannot separate to let just *one* word pass. A single word that would say 'you' or me'. Or 'equals'; she who loves, she who is loved. Closed and open, neither ever excluding the other, they say they both love each other.
>
> (1999, p. 84)

Moreover, Sappho's poems also answer Cixous's exhortation in 'The Laugh of the Medusa' to women to take up writing and inscribe their own subjectivity and desire:

> Woman must write herself: must write about women and bring women to writing, from which they have been driven away as violently as from their bodies – for the same reasons, by the same law. Woman must put herself into the text – as into the world and into history – by her own movement.
>
> (Cixous, 1981, p. 245)

Like Cixous's writing, Sappho's writing is powerfully utopian and subversive of phallocentric discourse. Indeed, Sappho and Sophia's love stands as an example of an absolute value and is contrasted with the commodified nature of contemporary romance criticized in *Written on the Body*. Sappho also stands as the unifying figure among the text's many fragmented parts; as Winterson observed, 'She holds the book together through her commentary and her reasoning and also her emotional power, which is eventually what brings the book to a proper close, finishes it' (Wachel, 1997, p. 68).

From the reader's perspective, the conclusion to this complex text is undoubtedly the most difficult to interpret of all Winterson's novels. On one level, the novel's fragmented stories come together when, at the end, the three characters get off the train they have been travelling on by the cliffs at Lesbos. The histories they divulge provide resolution of sorts as it transpires that Sappho's lover 'Sophia' is indeed Picasso, the baby Handel helps the young Spanish woman give birth to after she has been raped by Picasso's stepfather. However, throughout the text there is strong evidence that all three characters are in fact dead and the reader's gradual realization that this is an afterlife journey through the world of art and the imagination makes for a decidedly unsettling, if not bleak, resolution. As Onega points out, their journey represents the mythical descent into the underworld, 'the dwelling place of all dead writers and artists whose works have contributed to shaping a given culture' (2006, p. 145). Significantly, their words are represented as three voices and, as they talk, they appear to harmonize in the manner of a musical trio, thus moving them ineluctably from the 'temporal' realm of physical reality to the 'eternal' realm of music. In this respect, it seems fitting that the novel ends with nine pages of the score for Strauss' *Der Rosenkavalier* as the protagonists learn to heal their broken psyches, and begin to sing, both literally and metaphorically.[3] As Carpenter avers, 'They are learning to read themselves through the unravellings and re-readings of their pasts' (2007, p. 76), drawing on the skills they used in life: poetry for Sappho, painting for Picasso and singing for Handel.

ROMANCING SCIENCE: *GUT SYMMETRIES*

Like *Art & Lies*, *Gut Symmetries* is a highly experimental text, which blends different forms and styles of writing. The novel concerns a triangular relationship between a man and two women who narrate the story. Jove is a physicist working on GUT, the Grand Unified Theory of the title. He is married to a poet, Stella, and is having an affair with a research student, Alice. The novel charts what happens when the two women find out about each other, exploring the nature of love and desire, the differences between the sexes, attitudes to marriage and infidelity, and the blurring of roles that takes place in their 'infernal triangle' (*GS*, p. 37). This 'voice of lyric love' is just one strand in what Katy Emck has described as the 'three voices' of Jeanette Winterson, the other two being the 'fairground conjuring act' that refers to Winterson's incorporation of fantasy and magic realism and the 'human textbook' that represents the theories of the body, desire, reality and storytelling associated with postmodernism (1997, p. 21).

The novel explores a range of postmodern ideas about the binary structure of Western thought, the relationship between history, storytelling and the 'real', and the fluid nature of time, identity and desire. It pits a range of competing scientific, philosophical and mystical discourses against each other in a literary experiment to find patterns and correspondences within difference. On the mystical side of the binary, these include the deck of tarot cards (which provide the chapter headings) and the Jewish religion of Kabbalah, which is practised by Stella's father. On the scientific side, represented by Jove's and Alice's professions, are ranged the Theory of Relativity, Quantum Physics, Superstring Theory and Chaos Theory, the implications of which have been a radical challenge to traditional Newtonian science, in which physical objects behave in predictable ways according to natural and physical laws of motion. In contrast to the Newtonian model, states Winterson, everything about our world, both the parts of it we can see and the parts we cannot, is perpetually 'in motion' (GS, p. 9). Extending this idea to her own life, and the difficulty of biographical anchoring, Alice observes, 'What should be stable, shifts. What I am told is solid, slips. The sensible strong ordinary world of fixity is a folklore' (p. 10). This eminently postmodern discourse of ontological uncertainty is made to resonate with the post-Einsteinian theories of the universe as Winterson traces the 'symmetries' between the two.

The central idea of the novel is the 'GUT' or Grand Unified Theory, which refers to the search for a theory to unite the insights from contemporary scientific theories of the cosmos. As Grice and Woods explain,

> Gut Symmetries involves an extended pun on 1) the twentieth-century search for a 'Grand Unified Theory' (a 'GUT') of scientific forces in theoretical physics, begun with Einstein and continued today in the discoveries of 'Superstring Theory'; and 2) 'gut feelings', or something felt in the gut, i.e. intuitively.
>
> (Grice and Woods, 2007, p. 36)

From Superstring Theory, Winterson takes the idea that there is no First Principle and hence no solid basis to reality. She also draws on the ideas of non-linear causation, systems out of equilibrium, and discontinuous change described by Chaos Theory. Quantum Theory, which concerns the proliferation of uncertainty and allows for multiple chances, appears to lend credence to Winterson's view that 'space is not simply connected. History is not unalterable. The universe itself is forked' (GS, p. 160). She continues, 'In a quantum universe, heaven and hell are simply parallel possibilities [and] particles can hold positions contradictory and simultaneous' (p. 160). Whereas the unit of atomic physics is the particle, the unit of subatomic physics is the wave. Commenting on the connection between these seemingly conflicting explanations, Winterson asks, 'How can we be an entity (particle) and a wave?' and comes to the conclusion that 'we are and are not our bodies' (p. 162). In bringing together diverse discourses, Winterson attempts to find correspondences between different realities and epistemologies, musing on the connections between the paradoxes of the ancient Kabbalah and those of the new physics, for example: 'What physicists identify as our wave function may be what has traditionally been called the soul' (p. 161). As in all her 1990s works, she uses science to explore desire, and fiction to explore the human ramifications of science.

Developing a key theme of her 1980s work, that of non-linear notions of time, Winterson here explores scientific theories of temporality, contrasting the older linear notion of time as an arrow with the more complex Einsteinian concept of time as a river:

> Time.
> Newton visualised time as an arrow flying towards its target. Einstein understood time as a river, moving forward, forceful, directed, but also bowed, curved, sometimes subterranean, not ending but pouring itself into a greater sea.
>
> (p. 104)

This has implications for personal experience as Alice acknowledges: 'Past. Present. Future. The rational divisions of the rational life. And always underneath, in dreams, in recollections, in the moment of hesitation on a busy street, the hunch that life is not rational, not divided. That the mirrored compartments could break' (p. 20). And one of these compartments, human identity, is represented in the novel as fluid, unstable, shifting and fragmented:

> What or who? I cannot name myself . . . Is that me in the shop-glass? Is that me in the family photo? Is that me in the office window? Is that me in the silvered pages of a magazine? Is that me in the broken bottles

on the street? Everywhere I go, reflection. Everywhere a caught image of who I am. In all of that who am I?

(p. 12)

Perhaps owing to the instability of identity, names become highly symbolic in the novel: Jove's 'god of war' features alongside Stella's 'star' and Alice's various aliases including her 'real' name, Alluvia ('that which is deposited by a river' (p. 117)). Boats are significant too: Jove and Alice meet on the QE2; Stella and Jove go yachting in the Med, and Alice is born on a Mersey tugboat, recalling Winterson's previous water-dwelling heroine, Villanelle, the boatman's daughter from *The Passion*. Stella's story begins in 1947 when she is born on a sledge in a frozen New York to a Jewish mystic father and a German immigrant mother. Jove, born in Rome in 1940, is also a New York immigrant. He tells Alice the story of his life:

The bright boy who loves and hates America. Loves it because it has given him everything. Hates it because it has given him everything. The ambivalence of the immigrant everywhere.

(p. 96)

As these 'origin' stories suggest, Winterson's novel addresses a central theme of contemporary literature: the immigrant experience. But while Winterson references a range of cultural histories in the post-war world – Italian, Jewish, Northern working class – it would be more accurate to say that she explores imaginary migrations, journeys and border crossings, rather than particular immigrant experiences. Like Venice in *The Passion*, New York is here a 'city of invention and reinvention', in which 'the autobiography of the immigrant . . . re-writes itself as fiction' (p. 168). Moreover, the fantastic is never far from the story, featuring here in the conceit that Stella is born with a diamond lodged in her spine, after her mother swallowed it while pregnant. The magical Jewish girl turns out to be Jove's future wife. Alice is the daughter of a Liverpudlian self-made millionaire and grows up in the 1960s Liverpool in the grip of Beatlemania. The sometimes comic representation of family life as dysfunctional and eccentric is reminiscent of *Oranges* and the novel extends the critique of heterosexual marriage she started there. Adopting the image of the tower derived from the tarot pack of cards, Winterson represents marriage variously as a trophy, a talismanic symbol and a shattered fortress (*GS*, p. 40). With a pill-popping, unfaithful father and a disappointed, alcoholic mother, the 1950s marriage of Alice's parents is depicted as dysfunctional and unequal. By the end of the novel, it emerges that Alice's father was in love with Stella's mother and so the adulterous triangle stretches back to an earlier generation and is played out by Jove, Stella and Alice. The two women change the story, however, by going off together and abandoning the heterosexual imperative.

The novel sets up a series of binary oppositions between science and mysticism, rational thought and gut feeling, the material and the metaphysics, male and female in a manner reminiscent of Hélène Cixous's essay 'Sorties'. In each binary, the male term maps onto the privileged rational position and the female one onto the subordinated second term. Like Cixous's, Winterson's text performs an inversion by privileging Stella's more poetic, 'spiritual' narrative over Jove's more rational, masculine one. However, rather than move to the next step and deconstruct the opposition altogether, Grice and Woods argue that Winterson retains the binary structure: 'The engendering of science versus mystery in *Gut Symmetries* is a wholly stereotypical gendered structure that certainly does not escape from patriarchal notions of the male as a rigorous thinker, and the female as a vaguely impressionistic feeler' (2007, p. 39).

In a striking move, Winterson maps these oppositions onto the love triangle between Stella, Jove and Alice. Through Jove and Stella, the novel contrasts masculine and feminine perspectives on adultery, frequently using the format of the play script in order to dramatize the archetypal nature of the protagonists' three-way relationship: 'HE: Why do you confuse love and sex? SHE: Why do you continuously separate them?' (*GS*, p. 184). Yet, in a significant break with tradition Winterson rewrites the conventional adultery plot from the perspective of *both* the mistress *and* the wife. Discovering Alice's affair with Jove, Stella voices her feelings of hurt, anger and jealousy as a host of sexual images come unbidden into her head, the image of sky-diving and the loss of punctuation and grammar reflecting her sense of dissolution in the face of Jove's betrayal:

> I have become my own pornographer. His body. Her body. My body. Unseparated, twisting, dark . . . The silent gravity-gone somersault of she on he on she. There we are, the infernal triangle, turning in the lubricious air, breasts, cock, cunt, oversized, inflated parachutes of skin.I know we are falling, all three, but the ground is still a long way off. Until we grab each other like sky-divers. He was me I was him are we her?
>
> (p. 37)

Gut Symmetries provides Winterson's most explicit depiction of heterosexual sex thus far. She represents the male as decidedly phallic – Jove is no Jordan – but arguably challenges conventional representations of penetration, presenting it from Alice's point of view as connectedness rather than phallic mastery, apparently mirroring the sympathetic symmetry of the cosmos, as when Alice describes her passion for Jove: 'Kiss him and I kiss the full of him and the dust of him' (p. 101). However, as their relationship develops, Alice increasingly feels used by Jove, observing 'I thought he made me fully human. I did not think of him as one man and his dog' (p. 104), and eventually she leaves him for Stella, substituting lesbian for heterosexual love. Moreover, Stella presents the heterosexual love relationship more negatively, describing it in the language of invasion and capture.

Utilizing a scientific metaphor for the love triangle, Winterson compares the three of them to the three fundamental forces of 'The Standard Model: weak force, strong force and electromagnetic force', explaining that difficulties 'begin when these three separate forces are arbitrarily welded together' *His wife, his mistress, met*' (p. 97). Yet, when they finally meet at the Algonquin Hotel in New York, Alice is astonished to find herself no longer seeing Stella as the rival, the other woman of myth, but identifying *with* her and being seduced *by* her: 'What I did was outside of anything I had imagined I would do. I leaned across and kissed her' (p. 116). Lesbianism is represented as the unprecedented, unpredictable quantum event. Winterson's representation of their relationship suggests a mirroring or 'twinning' (Lewis, 1996): 'The reflective image of a woman with a woman is seductive' (*GS*, p. 119) and invokes Luce Irigaray's (1999) concept of the 'two lips' as an encounter with the self-same.

Grice and Woods (1998) have argued that the novel replaces a logic of (heterosexual) difference with a logic of the (lesbian) same. However, Winterson is careful to distinguish the lesbian relationship from narcissism *tout court*. In fact she represents lesbianism as a relationship simultaneously of sameness *and* difference; as Alice states, 'Her breasts as my breasts, her mouth as my mouth, were *more* than Narcissus hypnotized by his likeness . . . It was not myself I fell in love with it was her' (*GS*, p. 119, my emphasis). Drawing on an older model of 'science' as alchemy, Winterson represents their love affair as an experiment in 'alchemical transformations' (p. 102) as each woman charts the shift from a heterosexual relationship with Jove to a lesbian one with each other: 'Now that I have discovered you' (p. 103). In this respect, Terry Castle's (1990) notion of the 'counter-plot' of lesbian fiction provides a useful explanation for the way in which the novel replaces the conventional heterosexual triadic relationship of husband, wife and other woman with a lesbian dyad between Stella and Alice by means of dropping the male term.

The novel also foregrounds contrasting attitudes to 'eating the other' which correspond to sexual subject positions: when Stella first hears of the affair, she determines to 'eat' Alice as Jove has done and then 'spit her out' (*GS*, p. 29). However, as she falls in love with Alice her attitude to 'eating' her changes: 'Put your hand to my mouth. Kiss me. Tongue, teeth, words' (p. 173). Jove, as the spurned male, tries to separate the women through intimidation and mockery. 'What did you think you were playing at?' (p. 128), he shouts at Alice. 'I didn't think we were playing chess', she replies (p. 128). In a dramatic finale set at sea, he finally takes revenge on Stella by attempting to cannibalize her in a grotesque parody of the wedding vow, 'Til death do us part': 'I parted the flesh from the bone and I ate it' (p. 196). Whereas Jove's 'eating' of the women is destructive, Stella's and Alice's 'eating' of each other is regenerative.

Despite her disclaimers about the term, the novel is among Winterson's most explicitly 'lesbian' works: unusually, it does not occlude the ending, but delivers a happy resolution for the two women lovers as Stella is rescued from the boat and reunited with Alice. The text articulates the social taboo against lesbianism and registers the women's fear of homophobic categorization: 'Who-ever saw us would say, "There's a couple of . . ." ' (p. 118). Echoing the debate about sexual reproduction in *Sexing*, the novel offers a challenge to evolutionary theories of sexual attraction: 'Would it be natural?', Alice wonders, 'There is no biological necessity to want you . . . I do not want to reproduce myself . . .' (p. 127), yet she asserts her 'right' to love another woman. No doubt, as Grice and Woods aver, the novel 'sometimes loses itself in the trickeries of its playful parallels, and ultimately produces a narrative that falls apart rather than together' (2007, p. 36). Yet, despite these misgivings, Winterson pulls off a bold re-scripting of the romance genre and, at times, succeeds in pulling together the fragments into a richly poetic, Gaia-inspired vision of the 'symmetry of the universe':

> The separateness of our lives is a sham. Physics, mathematics, music, painting, my politics, my love for you, my work, the star-dust of my body, the spirit that impels it, clocks diurnal, time perpetual, the roll, rough, tender, swamping, liberating, breathing, moving, thinking nature, human nature and the cosmos are patterned together.
>
> (*GS*, p. 98)

5

THE POWERBOOK, LIGHTHOUSEKEEPING AND *WEIGHT*

I: 'HERE'S THE STORY': *THE POWERBOOK*

Just as her 1990s fiction exploited the possibilities suggested by the new physics, Winterson's first novel of the new millennium, as its name suggests, explores the implications for identity and narrative posed by the new computer technologies. *The PowerBook* flaunts its contemporaneousness on every page with chapter headings such as 'open hard drive', 'new document' and 'empty trash'. Set simultaneously in cyberspace and 'meatspace' – Paris, Capri and London – it takes Winterson's familiar exploration of multiple realities and personae into virtual reality, mapping the abandonment of the self that cyberspace makes possible. Indeed, the novel's very structure reflects the non-linear nature of reading hypertext and the mobility and mutability of online identities. Stretching Winterson's postmodern aesthetic to its limits, and pursuing her metafictional agenda of frame-breaking to a greater extent than previously, *The PowerBook* is a book in which the writing of the story *is* the story. As the narrator tells us throughout the text, 'I can change the story. I am the story' (pp. 5, 243). According to the author, the novel represents the end of her first cycle of works (Reynolds and Noakes, 2003, p. 25), a claim with which Keulks concurs in his view of the text:

> Overweighed with references to electronic communication, performative identity, and virtual reality, *The PowerBook* eludes even the most assimilative forms of realism that have recently been proposed. It is

her last full-fledged, first-phase postmodern novel, one that continues to thwart fixed conceptions of autonomy and agency – the dual crises of the postmodern self.

(2007, p. 148)

The novel's narrator is a writer who advertises her work on the Internet and offers customers a bespoke story in which they can be anyone they desire. A Scheherezade figure who sits at her laptop and tells us, 'To avoid discovery I stay on the run' (*PB*, p. 3), Ali/Alix is, like the narrator of *Written on the Body*, ambiguously gendered and appears in her e-narratives, by turns, female and male. Starting with the marvellous story of the cross-dressed Ali and her tulips, the narrator composes a romance for a female customer involving a love affair in Paris, Capri and London which, in a metafictional twist, becomes the 'real story' against which numerous inset tales are set. These are drawn from a variety of sources including Arthurian legend, medieval romance and fairy tale. In particular, the novel retells the archetypal love stories of Lancelot and Guinevere (from Malory's *Morte D'Arthur*), and Paulo and Francesca (from texts by Boccaccio and Dante). In addition, the text makes numerous references to 'great and ruinous lovers', both heterosexual and gay, such as Romeo and Juliet, Tristan and Isolde, Vita and Virginia, and Oscar and Bosie. Significantly, all of the stories are about either illicit or obsessive love and its (usually fatal) consequences. In one of these, a beautifully told tale based on the Medieval Italian source, Francesca falls in love with the manservant, Paulo, who is charged with bringing Francesca to her intended husband, a grotesque dwarf, named Giancotto. After the marriage the pair becomes lovers once more, but they are discovered by Giancotto, who impales them on a lance as they make love. Another archetypal tale begins: 'A hunter loved a princess. Simple as that' (p. 179). The princess asks the hunter to bring her the pelt of a red fox she covets. Against his will he does so but asks that its life be spared. However, the princess has her servant kill it whereupon it turns into the hunter, lying dead on the snow. Throughout these tales of passion runs the refrain: 'There is no love that does not pierce the hands and feet' (p. 128). Despite superficial differences, the narrator tells us with a nod to Vladimir Propp's (1968) study of folk tales, the basic structure is always the same: 'always this story' (*PB*, p. 119).

Back in the frame narrative, meanwhile, Ali's seduction of her customer through stories turns into something more as she falls in love with her, and the line between the frame narrative and the inset tales begins to blur. When the customer-lover suddenly disappears, the narrator keeps writing in the hope that the lover will respond. She begins to tell the story in different ways. Now, her aim is to 'Break the narrative. Refuse all the stories. Try to tell the story differently' (p. 53). As the narrator tells us, 'Love's script has no end of beginnings. The characters and the scenery change. There are three possible endings: Revenge. Tragedy. Forgiveness' (pp. 77–78). Loath to repeat the narrative of lost or unrequited love, and desperate for a happy ending, the narrator retells the story in multiple ways and in different genres, one leading on to the next like a set of Russian 'matryoshka' dolls. In a key statement of the novel, the author-narrator informs us, 'I keep telling this story – different people, different places, different times – but always you, always me, always this story, because a story is a tightrope between two worlds' (p. 119). This image of the tightrope is repeated at intervals throughout the novel (pp. 166, 210) and recalls the aerialism of Winterson's other fictional heroines such as *The Passion*'s Fortunata.

The novel is full of intertextual allusions to Winterson's previous work. As in her 1990s novels, the beloved is a beautiful, married redhead who has to choose between married security and the narrator's riskier proposition. Winterson reworks the seduction scene between Alice and Stella in *Gut Symmetries* in which Alice, narrating, kisses Stella (*GS*, p. 116); this time 'she leaned forward and kissed me' (*PB*, p. 42). When the customer turned lover asks Ali about the story she is writing, Ali tells her it is about boundaries and desire, and when the lover asks 'What are your other books about?' Winterson, in a humorous allusion to her own work, has Ali reply, 'Boundaries. Desire' (p. 35).[1] The technique of frame-breaking is used to dizzying effect in the novel: in the Paris section, Ali and the lover visit 'Ali's', a Turkish café, which refers back to the inset tale in the opening section. 'That was just a story', the customer complains of the narrator's Ali and the tulip tale. 'This is just a story', she/he replies (p. 27). 'What happened to the omniscient author?', she asks. 'Gone interactive' (p. 27), the narrator quips back. In another metafictional allusion to the status of the tales, the lover responds to Ali's stories of doomed love by demanding, 'Is this how the story ends? [...] You could rewrite the story. Isn't there a better ending than either/or?' (p. 133).

Rewriting the story is of course what Winterson has been doing since *Oranges*, and *PowerBook* includes a striking version of the origin story first told there, about a young girl brought up by an unhappy and superstitious adoptive family. The Muck House is a grotesque version of Winterson's Accrington home: the house is full of scrap and rubbish and little Alix's bed is a cattle trough. It is run on strictly utilitarian lines: she is tolerated because 'girls are cheaper, easier, cleaner' (*PB*, p. 138), but reading and writing are forbidden because 'there's no use for words here' (p. 141). Her parents tell her there is no other world beyond the scrap yard, but in common with other Wintersonian heroes/heroines, Alix is a quest figure who comes to the realization that 'I had to find the treasure' (p. 146) and 'In this life you have to be your own hero' (p. 155). Moreover, Winterson provides a poignant rationale for storytelling in (her own) abandonment: 'They gave me away' (p. 156), commenting that 'Life was a journey I would have to make by myself' (p. 156). Storytelling is thus a means of both putting the self into discourse and covering up an original lack or absence.

Elsewhere, Ali gives an alternative rationale for her urge to tell stories: 'I live in one world – material, seeming solid – and the weight of that is quite enough' (p. 54). Stories therefore serve as a means of escape from the burdens of identity, as a way of keeping the world 'light'. They offer 'multiple possibilities' like 'maps of journeys that have been made and might have been made' (p. 53). Moreover, as the novel's many quest narratives gradually reveal, stories are at their simplest a means of narrativizing desire: 'My search for you, your search for me, is a search after something that cannot be found' (p. 78). Winterson here returns to the idea of treasure from *The Passion* – 'the valuable, fabulous thing' (*P*, p. 98). The end of the novel makes this clear as Winterson collapses all the various love stories into one archetypal quest narrative, which appears to return the romance to its medieval roots: a hero fighting his way through the forest in search of the object of desire, whether this be 'his lady, his falcon, [or] his horse' (*PB*, p. 239). This idea of story as a (potentially infinite) quest accords with Jacques Lacan's (1977) model of desire as a chain of signifiers in which the final signified and therefore meaning is endlessly deferred – 'The palace was deserted' (*PB*, p. 238); 'All [the rooms] were empty' (p. 239) – but we are impelled onwards neverthe-less. Human desire, and the stories that give it symbolic meaning, represents the quest for the 'treasure'.

Ali herself is presented as a fiction, a figure that slips through the gaps of history. 'Ali tells stories for a living', we are told, and 'the stories are telling him' (p. 215). Discourse is constitutive of real-ity and identity: 'What he is, what he invents, becomes part of the same story' (p. 216). The magic carpet from the tale of Ali Baba and the 40 thieves becomes a metaphorical carpet in which Ali weaves his past and his future and, by extension, Winterson weaves her fictions. Fiction and reality become interchangeable: 'I am sitting at my screen reading this story. In turn, the story reads me' (p. 209). But, as the narrator acknowledges, while the story can be perfect in fantasy, 'downloaded into real life, it was messy' (p. 46). At this point, the embedded narrative has become thoroughly indistin-guishable from the frame story of the narrator and her customer. As in Winterson's other works, the boundary between 'reality' and 'fiction' is shown to be fluid and permeable. The journey through cyberspace leads to a blurring of boundaries between self and other, real and imagined, writing and reading. For just as the nar-rator emails her lover, so her e-novel calls her into being, creating her identity discursively: 'The story is reading you now, line by line' (p. 84). This idea accords with the post-structuralist notion that identity is constructed in and through discourse and that we are subjects-in-process (Kristeva, 1986, p. 91). The story becomes transitive, not just something that passes between readers, but something that actively writes itself and 'reads' its readers.

The PowerBook foregrounds simultaneously the mutability and the limitations of identity. Responding to the customer's desire to change identity, the narrator offers the chance of 'scrolling into another self' (*PB*, p. 103), and discarding the corporeal body in favour of a metaphorical body of stories:

You say you want to be transformed.

This is where the story starts. Here, in these long lines of laptop DNA. Here we take your chromosomes, twenty-three pairs, and alter your height, eyes, teeth, sex. This is an invented world. You can be free just for one night.

Undress.

> Take off your clothes. Take off your body. Hang them up behind the
> door. Tonight we can go deeper than disguise.
>
> (p. 4)

The text demonstrates the possibilities presented by the Internet for shucking off old identities and adopting new ones. Ali's e-writer anticipates the pleasures of popular interactive games such as *Second Life*, in which you can fabricate a new persona complete with bespoke lifestyle.[2] This conceit enables Winterson to peel back the layers of 'the self' beyond both cultural gender and biological sex. The novel exemplifies Winterson's belief, expressed throughout her work, that 'we think of ourselves as closed and finite, when we are multiple and infinite' (p. 103).

The cyberspace motif facilitates an exploration of this postmodern concept of subjectivity in terms of the new technologies, comparing the self to a 'windows' programme:

> There are so many lives packed into one. The one life we think we know is only the window that is open on the screen. The big window full of detail, where the meaning is often lost among the facts. If we can close that window, on purpose or by chance, what we find behind is another view.
>
> (p. 103)

The structure of the text approximates to a series of 'windows', each adding a layer to the narrative so that reading it is analogous to surfing the web. Through a series of metafictional interventions, Winterson makes the surfing–writing–reading analogy explicit:

> When I sit at my computer, I accept that the virtual worlds I find there parallel my own. I talk to people whose identity I cannot prove. I disappear into a web of co-ordinates that we say will change the world. What world? Which world?
>
> (pp. 93–94)

Winterson's use of the web as a tool to transcend and evade sexual difference while proliferating and celebrating sexuality engages with the aspect of contemporary 'third wave' feminism known as cyberfeminism. In particular, *The PowerBook* exhibits what Donna Haraway calls the 'pleasure in the confusion of boundaries' (1990, p. 191), both sexual and textual. Winterson's postmodern representation of identity may also be understood in terms of Zoe Sofia's (1999) concept of 'virtual corporeality', an oxymoron suggesting an impossible combination. *The PowerBook*'s transsexual time-traveller Ali/Alix is another version of the gender and species hybrids that populate her other novels. The novel answers Haraway's call for texts 'in a postmodern, nonnaturalist mode and in the utopian tradition of imagining a world without gender' (Haraway, 1990, p. 192), and appears to concur with Sadie Plant's (1999) view that computer technology offers an alternative to gender binarism. When asked her sex online, for example, the narrator responds 'Does it matter? This is a virtual world' (*PB*, p. 26).

Nevertheless there are moments in the text which seem to privilege the material body of 'meatspace', and when a more specifically 'lesbian' discourse is foregrounded. One such moment is when Ali's lover comes to London to see her in her Spitalfields home and they make love:

> Sex between women is mirror geography. The subtlety of its secret – utterly the same, utterly different. You are a looking-glass world. You are the hidden place that opens to me on the other side of the glass. I touch your smooth surface and then my fingers sink through to the other side. You are what the mirror reflects and invents. I see myself, I see you, two, one, none. I don't know. Maybe I don't need to know. Kiss me.
>
> (p. 174)

Recalling the 'twinning' discourse utilized in *Art & Lies* and *Gut Symmetries*, which drew on Irigaray's concept of the 'two lips' (1999), Winterson plays on the Freudian model of lesbianism as narcissism, a form of mimicry that risks fixing lesbianism as a form of self-love, and thus eliding the differences between women. However, as in the earlier novels, Winterson also foregrounds the physical attraction between self and other; as Ali wryly comments, 'Meatspace still has some advantages for a carbon-based girl' (p. 174).

This emphasis on bodily experience provides an important critique of disembodied forms of postmodernism and, in particular, cyberculture's celebration of bodilessness. Discussing the place of the body in contemporary cultural discourse, Ina Schabert argues that the 'latest victory of mind over corporeal matter has been gained in cyberspace', and the old mind/body dichotomy of Enlightenment thought is reinforced rather than challenged in 'the formal separation of the user's mind from the body or bodies, or body parts he makes use of on the net' (2001, p. 93). Schabert interprets Winterson's use of body writing metaphors as an attempt to deconstruct the opposition between mind and body by 'pres[sing] the disembodied mode of writing into the service of presenting, representing, "re-membering" and reliving the body' (2001, p. 87). Winterson's treatment of the body may therefore be seen to represent a rejection of cyberculture's more conservative and disembodied stance. The novel ends with a reference to a pictorial book: 'Your Body is my Book of Hours. Open it. Read it' (PB, p. 243). Interestingly, as Schabert comments, medieval illuminated manuscripts used the metaphor of the book of the body to 'convey the inseparability of body and soul, of physical existence and intimately personal meaning' (2001, p. 107). This is precisely how Winterson utilizes the body/text metaphor in her own attempt to write the body and make the word flesh.

Finally, relinquishing authorial responsibility, the ending of the novel passes it over to the reader, providing alternative conclusions reminiscent of John Fowles's The French Lieutenant's Woman. 'Here are two endings. You choose' (PB, p. 205), the narrator insists. In the first one, Ali jumps off the train taking her lover to Oxford as the whistle blows, pleading with her lover to follow. In the second ending, she is joined on the platform by her lover who abandons her bag on the train. For Keulks, 'this ending is defeatist and decidedly postmodernist; it threatens to swamp Ali's desire for integrity in excessive signification', and demonstrates 'that escape can be at best transitory in a world of postmodern performativity, textuality, and disconnection' (2007, p. 150). However, this is not quite the end: several chapters follow in which Ali goes back to her computer to 'write the story again' (PB, p. 243). While the reader is unsure whether to read the final image of the lovers, 'a pair of twins spun out of constellation' (p. 231), as real or imagined, past or present, we accept it as part of the story. And while the novel ends ambiguously, with no clear resolution to the love affair, it does nevertheless affirm the value of the quest. Moreover, in the image of the river's silt, there is a move, at the end of the novel, towards a more material sense of historical reality. Silt, neither solid nor liquid, represents an apt metaphor for Winterson's concept of history as a process of continual shifting and settling, arguably moving it beyond the purely textual:

> Perhaps this is how it is – life flowing smoothly over memory and history, the past returning or not, depending on the tide. History is a collection of found objects washed up through time. Goods, ideas, personalities surface towards us, then sink away. Some we hook out, others we ignore, and as the pattern changes, so does the meaning.
>
> (p. 242)

After *The PowerBook*, as we shall see, Winterson increasingly turns her attention to what she calls 'the weight of accumulation' (*PB*, p. 54), of history and selfhood. If her work up to this point has largely concerned enabling escapes from the past and the rejection of 'identity' as an unnecessary burden, hereafter, Winterson begins to explore if not embrace rootedness and responsibility to a much greater extent.

KEEPING THE LIGHT: *LIGHTHOUSEKEEPING*

In *Lighthousekeeping* there are similarities to previous works, parallel narratives set in different periods, a girl narrator reminiscent of Jeanette in *Oranges*, and an ongoing intertextual meditation on the themes of identity, love and storytelling. However, according to the author, *Lighthousekeeping* initiates 'a new exploration', representing the first text in a new cycle of works (*L*, Appendix, p. 3). The novel explores new ground, most notably drawing back from the uncompromising postmodern aesthetic of recent texts and going some way towards reinstating a sense of linear history, topographical setting and character motivation, all concepts jettisoned by Winterson's high postmodernist novels. In contrast to *The PowerBook*, Keulks argues that *Lighthousekeeping* tries 'to refigure postmodernism for the inescapably historical, serious, and decidedly *un*-ironic twenty-first century' and reveals 'the first example of a restrained and moderated, potentially new Wintersonian voice' (2007, p. 148). In particular, the novel introduces a stronger narrative thread than has been evident for some time in Winterson's fiction and, as some broadsheet critics commented, it provides readerly pleasures more reminiscent of her early work through its poignant stories of love and loss (Briscoe, 2004).

The novel is narrated by an orphan named Silver, who, as her name suggests, is 'part precious metal, part pirate' (*L*, p. 3). Like Jeanette in *Oranges*, Silver is reared by an unconventional and highly religious mother who insists on her difference and tells her, 'If you can't survive in this world, you'd better make a world of your own' (p. 5). Winterson describes their life together in the imaginary Scottish town of Salts with characteristic humour and inventiveness: 'My home-town. A sea-flung, rock-bitten sand-edged shell of a town. Oh, and a lighthouse' (p. 5). The casual reference to the lighthouse is ironic: it is of course the dominant motif of the novel. The description of the house cut into a steep hill, in which 'the chairs had to be nailed to the floor and we were never allowed to eat spaghetti' (p. 3), also recalls the magical city without gravity in *Sexing the Cherry* and, like Jordan, Silver dreams 'of a place where I wouldn't be fighting gravity with my own body weight' (p. 4). On the death of her mother, and after an interlude at the dreadful Miss Pinch's house, Silver is apprenticed to Pew, a blind lighthousekeeper who teaches her how 'to keep the light', but more importantly how to 'tell yourself as a story' (p. 27) and how to love another human being. Ultimately, Pew and Silver are forced to leave the lighthouse when automation is introduced. Silver embarks on a lonely search for love and meaning, travelling first to Bristol in search of Pew and then abroad – to Capri and Athens – to escape from her own 'darkness'. As Keulks (2007) points out, she continues the *flâneuse* tradition of female wanderers in Winterson's work. Following a 20-year gap in which Silver has a nervous breakdown and starts a relationship with an unnamed female lover, the novel ends with Silver's return to the lighthouse and a reunion with Pew, who reaffirms both the importance of love and the power of stories.

In the course of the novel, Silver relates the history of the Cape Wrath lighthouse and the stories connected to it, including the story of Babel Dark, a nineteenth-century clergyman and the town's most famous resident since Charles Darwin came to visit him, in 1859. We learn that as a young man Dark fell in love with but then abandoned a woman named Molly, who went on to have his child. Thereafter, Dark became a minister and exiled himself to Salts. But one day he encounters Molly again by chance and begins a double life, spending ten months of the year in his Scottish parish unhappily married, and two months in Bristol with Molly and his child, a girl who like Silver is 'a child born of chance' (p. 32), and like Pew is born blind. While in Bristol Dark adopts the name 'Lux' and spends happy, light-filled days with Molly and her child. Dark's story reaches a climax when Molly, disguised as Mrs Tenebris, follows him to Salts and asks him to come away with her for good. Dark, however, betrays her love a second time and she leaves him for good. Heartbroken and wretched, he ends his life by walking into the sea.

Pew, the lighthousekeeper, is a timeless and magical figure who 'has the look of being there forever' (p. 15). Like the lighthouse itself Pew represents a stable point and the continuity of history; as he tells Silver, 'There has always been a Pew in the lighthouse at Cape Wrath' (p. 46). Blind from birth, he lives in darkness but 'keeps the light', both by tending the lighthouse and by telling stories. Pew tells Silver about illiterate sailors who could not read books or maps but 'read' places like stories: 'Every lighthouse has a story to it' (p. 39). He maintains the oral storytelling tradition and the knowledge it sustains. At his insistence, Silver learns both this and how to operate the lighthouse: 'That's what you must learn. Both the ones I know and the ones I don't know' (p. 40). Winterson develops the novel's refrain – 'keeping the light' – as a metaphor for storytelling: 'every light had a story – no, every light was a story, and the flashes themselves were the stories going out over the waves, as markers and guides and comfort and warning' (p. 41). Like the other blind seer Tiresius,[3] Pew bears witness to events, unites opposites and embodies contradictions: 'He was and he wasn't – that was Pew' (p. 95). He claims to have sailed in a ship that sank 200 years before and witnessed Dark's meeting with Molly. Silver is as disbelieving as the reader, but Winterson reminds the latter that stories are often about impossible things: 'the thing couldn't have happened, but it did' (p. 127).

Lighthousekeeping is structured by a whole series of binary oppositions – light/dark, fixity/fluidity, self/other, objective/subjective, male/female – which are mobilized, interrogated and subsequently deconstructed in the course of the novel. These binaries even underpin Winterson's style, which oscillates between factual and romantic descriptions:

> *Cape Wrath.* Position on the nautical chart, 58° 37.5° N, 5°W.
>
> Look at it – the headland is 368 feet high, wild, grand, impossible. Home to gulls and dreams.
>
> (p. 12)

The novel's central symbols, the lighthouse and the sea, represent the binary oppositions fixity and fluidity, which Winterson memorably describes, 'Look at this one. Made of granite, as hard and unchanging as the sea is fluid and volatile. The sea moves constantly, the lighthouse, never. There is no sway, no rocking, none of the motion of ships and ocean' (p. 17). Pew embodies both oppositions simultaneously: by virtue of his second sight he can see 'what's ebbing and what's becoming' (p. 48) and thereby represents the principle of fluidity. However, the lighthouse is also directly associated with him: 'It stood, Pew-shaped, Pew-still, hatted by cloud, blind-eyed, but the light to see by' (p. 95). While the lighthouse, as this reference to a blind-eyed tower suggests, is a characteristically phallic image, Winterson plays down its phallic connotations. Pew is a nurturing figure to Silver, and the lighthouse becomes her home, a 'safe space', 'a womb' (p. 32).

While Dark is compared to the lighthouse ('I stood firm' (p. 188)), Molly also represents a stabilizing force, 'a grounding rod' (p. 101). Moreover, in illuminating the passage of sailors, the lighthouse does so by flashing a light at four-second intervals, incorporating contrasting elements. 'The lighthouse is a known point in the darkness' (p. 38) for Silver and Pew: 'Our business was light, but we lived in darkness' (p. 20). The lighthouse is a polysemic sign, meaning different things at different times. In drawings by Stevenson, the lighthouse looks 'like a living creature, standing upright on its base, like a seahorse, fragile, impossible, but triumphant in the waves' (p. 80). Significantly, Dark is also compared to both a seahorse and the lighthouse (p. 119), suggesting fragility and solidity simultaneously. The text thus works to deconstruct the binary oppositions between lighthouse and sea, stability and fluidity, masculine and feminine.

As well as deconstructing binaries, *Lighthousekeeping* makes use of postmodern metafiction and intertextuality. At one point, having started her story several times at different points in history, Silver confesses, 'A beginning, a middle and an end is the proper way to tell a story. But I had trouble with that method' (*L*, p. 23). This metafictional device of false starts emphasizes the arbitrariness of narrative and the potentially limitless interconnections between stories. As Pew remarks, 'there's no story that's the start of itself' (p. 27). Despite the emphasis on storytelling then, the text repeatedly calls into the question the linearity and discreteness of narrative, ultimately eschewing realist principles. Postmodern intertextuality is pervasive. Characters are lifted from texts by others: Pew, the lighthousekeeper, Silver, the novel's female narrator, and DogJim, her pet, are named after the characters Blind Pew, Long John Silver and Jim Hawkins from Robert Louis Stevenson's children's adventure novel *Treasure Island*. The historical figures Charles Darwin and Robert Louis Stevenson are given speaking parts in the story, and the novel makes extensive intertextual allusion to a range of literary and scientific works including Darwin's *On the Origin of Species*, Stevenson's *The Strange Case of Dr Jekyll and Mr Hyde*, Doris Lessing's *The Golden Notebook*, E.M. Forster's *Howard's End* and, of course, Virginia Woolf's *To the Lighthouse*. The novel is permeated by a series of strange coincidences and uncanny parallels between fiction and fact: in 1828 the lighthouse is built by Robert Stevenson and Babel Dark is born. In 1850, Dark arrives in Salts and Robert Louis Stevenson is born. Later, his meeting with Babel inspires Stevenson to write *Jekyll and Hyde*. On his last day in the lighthouse, Pew leaves Silver a first edition copy of Darwin's *Origin of Species* and Stevenson's *Dr Jekyll and Mr Hyde* along with Babel Dark's diaries. Amidst the chaos of life, the text traces intertextual connections and seeks narrative symmetries.

In a clever reworking of Stevenson's classic tale *Dr Jekyll and Mr Hyde* Winterson adroitly reverses the intertextual relationship so that Stevenson's novel appears to have been inspired by Babel's own story. From Stevenson's narrative of split personality and estrangement, Winterson takes the theme of the otherness of human identity. The binaries, dark and light, are symbolized by the two selves of the protagonist, Babel Dark and his *alter ego*, Lux. Just as Dr Jekyll comes to recognize the 'primitive duality in man' (Stevenson, 2004, p. 49), Babel Dark comes to see himself as 'a stranger in my own life' (*L*, p. 64). He deals with this struggle by splitting himself into two, becoming 'this fractured man' (p. 84), using his status as dutiful minister to protect him and cover his tracks. However, in each case their two identities refuse to remain separate and discrete, and begin to cross over into each other's worlds. At this point in her narrative, Winterson directly quotes *Dr Jekyll and Mr Hyde* and draws the comparison between its tale of split personality and Babel Dark's double life: '"You understand me, Pew? I am Henry Jekyll." He paused for a moment, looking at his hands, strong, long and studious. "And I am Edward Hyde"' (p. 187), thereby intertextually invoking and reversing the moment in Stevenson's text when Jekyll looks down at his hand and realizes that he has woken as Hyde.

Like Henri in *The Passion*, Dark is a diarist, keeping two journals which reflect the two sides of his nature: a neat diary of his life as a minister, and 'a wild and torn folder of scattered pages' (*L*, p. 57). Later, Silver begins her own diary, writing in 'shiny silver notebooks' (p. 139), which alludes to the writing of Anna Wulf in Doris Lessing's novel *The Golden Notebook*. There are further intertextual connections. Anna is an alienated figure who suffers from mental illness and struggles to make sense of her place in the world, much like Winterson's characters. Anna keeps multiple notebooks which represent the different parts of herself, but unlike Dark, Anna is finally able to bring together these divided aspects of herself in the golden notebook. And just like *Lighthousekeeping*, *The Golden Notebook* contains numerous texts within texts and doubled fictional characters. Moreover, in its experimental form and radical politics, it has been seen as an early example of postmodern feminist writing.

Whatever the villainous Hyde got up to in Stevenson's tale, we know that Babel Dark's secret is his adulterous love for Molly; as Pew remarks, 'there's always a woman somewhere' (*L*, p. 73). But Winterson subverts Stevenson's original narrative by inverting the meanings of dark and light in her postmodern reworking: 'The obvious equation was Dark = Jekyll, Lux = Hyde. The impossible truth was that in his life it was the reverse' (p. 187). Dark is less like Jekyll, the upright doctor, and more like Hyde, the debased and hateful incarnation, an equation borne out by his abusive treatment of his wife. In contrast, Lux represents his better self, one who learns to love and trust another human being. The result, however, is as damaging as in Stevenson's tale: having kept Molly in the dark about his family in Salts, he betrays her a second time, and the strain of living two lives eventually leads him to take his own life. The moral of the story –'to avoid either extreme, it is necessary to find all the lives in between' (p. 161) – may be read as a plea to go beyond the binary and acknowledge the multiplicity of identity, as Woolf advocates in *To the Lighthouse*.

Although treated less explicitly than the engagement with *Dr Jekyll and Mr Hyde*, allusions to Woolf's 1927 novel permeate the text, providing not only the novel's title and its major motif, the lighthouse, but some of its major themes: life as a journey, human striving, longing and loss: 'There was only forward, northwards into the sea. To the lighthouse' (*L*, p. 19). Both *Lighthousekeeping* and *To the Lighthouse* are primarily concerned with the reconciliation of opposing principles, culminating in a momentous journey to a lighthouse and the completion of an artistic work. Winterson also shares Woolf's modernist privileging of subjective perception over the objective representation of external reality. For example, the appearance and meaning of Woolf's lighthouse are determined by the perception of the viewer: 'One can hardly tell which is the sea and which is the land' (Woolf, 2000, p. 119). Similarly, as we have seen, Winterson's lighthouse embodies different characteristics at different times. As home to the blind visionary Pew and the orphan Silver, the lighthouse is not so much a symbol of phallic mastery as a beacon 'calling you home' (*L*, p. 134), a place of safety and small domestic rituals. Yet, paradoxically, in a text of playful, shifting ironies, it is invoked as an absolute value: a fixed point in a turning world. Woolf's ending is decidedly modernist in that the travellers achieve their goal and Lily the painter completes her artwork: 'It was done, it was finished . . . I have had my vision' (Woolf, 2000, p.198). Winterson abjures such closure. 'There's no such thing as an ending' (*L*, p. 49), she writes; 'there is no continuous narrative, there are lit-up moments, and the rest is dark' (p. 134); and 'the story of life' is simply 'one that begins again' (p. 109).

The text identifies 1859 (100 years before Silver's – and Winterson's – birth) as a key date in Western history, marking the publication of Darwin's *Origin of Species* and the completion of Richard Wagner's opera *Tristan and Isolde*. Winterson presents these figures as representing two diametrically opposed poles of the culture: 'Darwin – objective, scientific, empirical, quantifiable. Wagner – subjective, poetic, intuitive, mysterious' (p. 169). The novel meditates on the possible reconciliation of these two poles. In a key episode, Babel Dark's dog falls down the Cliffside and, on rescuing him, Dark discovers a cave filled with fossils of ferns and seahorses, so significant a discovery for the study of natural history that Darwin himself comes to Salts to examine them (p. 19). What it demonstrates to an astonished Dark is that the universe is constantly evolving and transforming itself. However, Dark laments the loss of a stable, God-given world: 'That things might be endlessly moving was not his wish' (p. 119). Winterson's view of Darwinism emphasizes not so much the 'fixity' of scientific laws but the fluidity, variety and unpredictability of life that they point to: 'In nature, he found not past, present and future, as we recognise them, but an evolutionary process of change – energy trapped for too long – life always becoming' (p. 150). This is the same lesson that Pew teaches Silver: 'everything can be recovered, not as it was, but in its changing form' and 'nothing keeps the same form forever, child, not even Pew' (p. 150). The novel explores how we deal with the knowledge of a world constantly changing and our contradictory desires to stay the same.

Although not endorsing Babel's dark and mystical world view, the text nevertheless suggests that while evolution may explain the physical world, it cannot account for intangibles like human subjectivity and desire. As the narrator states,

> In the fossil record of our existence, there is no trace of love. You cannot find it held in the earth's crust, waiting to be discovered. The long bones of our ancestors show nothing of their hearts. Their last meal is sometimes preserved in peat or in ice, but their thoughts and feelings are gone.
>
> (p. 170)

It is the task of the storyteller – and the poet and the composer – to 'trace love'. Winterson therefore extends Darwin's theory of evolution, with its emphasis on the connections and relationships between species, to the nature of storytelling and texts themselves. And the novel may be read in terms of the fossil motif as representing a mapping of 'stories layered by time' (p. 39).

Within its various stories, the novel explores another set of binaries, the need to belong versus the desire to break free, constancy and familiarity versus difference and otherness. Life, for Silver, is a search *both* for a home or 'anchor', represented by the fixed point of the lighthouse, *and* for love and adventure, represented by the journeys she makes and the relationships she has. In the end, Winterson privileges the human bonds of love and offers E.M. Forster's famous dictum 'Only connect' as the novel's refrain. The novel affirms Pew's – and Winterson's – vision of stories as sustaining and life-affirming and, if the final image of Pew rowing away in his boat is an ambiguous one, leaving Silver alone and unanchored, the novel does nevertheless reverberate with memorable characters who affirm their relationship to each other and the world. Pew, as its chief storyteller, provides the moral 'message' of the novel: 'You must never doubt the one you love' (p. 85).

'ALWAYS BOUNDARIES AND DESIRE': *WEIGHT*

In many ways the novella *Weight* is a companion text to *Lighthousekeeping*. It explores similar themes of love, desire and the boundaries of self and world; and utilizes similar tropes drawn from Evolutionary Theory and Quantum Physics. It also foregrounds the theme of responsibility: in this case Atlas's 'impossible burden' (*W*, p. 89) of shouldering the world. Written for the Canongate *Myths* series, in which modern writers rework a myth in a contemporary way, Winterson's *Weight* retells the story of Atlas, the Titan, who wages war against the gods and is punished by being made to hold up the world, and of Heracles, the mythical strong man, who offers to take the weight – temporarily – from his shoulders. It therefore extends into mythology the exploration of what has become the defining theme of Winterson's work to date: 'boundaries, desire' (p. 131) and the limits of the self.

The myth allows Winterson to explore the contemporary theme of freedom of choice and self-determination in the Greek context of fate and destiny. Her retelling is an inventive, witty and imaginative recasting of an archetypal story. In the novella's prologue, Winterson carries over the tropes of river sediment from *The PowerBook* and of fossil remains from *Lighthousekeeping* to represent the accumulation of natural and, by extension, human history. According to Darwin, evolutionary history is legible in the layers of accumulated sediment. In drawing a metaphorical parallel between this image and the pages of a book, which contain a record of contemporary life that is yet 'far from complete' (*W*, p. xiv), Winterson introduces her familiar theme of the open-ended character of both textuality and human life, using differently sized fonts to suggest the evolutionary process. In the introduction explaining her selection of a myth to rework, Winterson extends the analogy between textuality and sexuality by stating that 'choice of subject, like choice of lover, is an intimate decision' (p. xvii). Interestingly, Winterson does not choose a female myth as Margaret Atwood (2005) did in her rewriting of Penelope's story. Rather, she was prompted to pick the Atlas myth because of the opportunities it affords to explore 'loneliness, isolation, responsibility, burden, and freedom' (*W*, p. xviii). In a conscious verbal echo of *The PowerBook*, she tells the reader that the recurring language motif of the novella is 'I want to tell the story again' (p. xviii). Reminding us that her work is full of cover versions, she also admits, 'Of course I wrote it out of my own situation. There is no other way' (p. xviii). As she has done repeatedly in interviews and essays, Winterson emphasizes the interpenetration of fiction and autobiography, and provides a valuable commentary on how she sees the relationship between the two: 'Autobiography is not important. Authenticity is important . . . Simply it is real' (p. xix). Winterson therefore reaffirms her belief in the power of storytelling and its 'mythic not its explanatory qualities', capable of revealing 'permanent truths about human nature' (p. xx).

The first chapter, aptly titled 'I want to tell the story again', provides an origin story of the universe, describing the beginnings of the world from nothing. In an allusion to *Gut Symmetries*, Winterson invokes 'light patterns of millennia opening in your gut' and observes 'your first parent was a star' (*W*, pp. 3–4).[4] As with the earlier novel, Winterson provides a scientific account of the universe, here describing it in terms of a chemical reaction in which the evolution of man was a chance event. Listing the variety of species in Darwinian fashion, she develops the image used at the end of *The PowerBook* and in *Lighthousekeeping*, describing the stories as 'silt-packed and fossil-stored' (*W*, p. 6). In playful, sexy prose Winterson describes Poseidon's – god of the sea – wooing of the Earth. Atlas is their offspring – half man, half god, one of the legendary Titans, whose name means 'the long-suffering one'. His brother is Prometheus and according to myth they both transgress, Prometheus by stealing fire from the gods, Atlas by fighting for freedom. Atlas's desire to 'get beyond' the story (p. 14) and his 'longing for infinite space' (p. 16) are another expression of a key Wintersonian theme: the desire to transcend boundaries, both existential and textual. And yet, unlike previous heroes/heroines – Jeanette, Villanelle, Jordan, Alice, Ali and Silver – Atlas is completely immobile, literally rooted to the spot by his 'monstrous burden', which is 'the boundary of what I am' (p. 21). The novella explores how he comes to terms with this situation.

Heracles, the son of the god Zeus and the mortal Alceme, is introduced as the 'hero of the world', the strongest man on earth and something of a thug: 'I was a bit of a braggart in my youth – killed everything, shagged what was left, and ate the rest' (*W*, pp. 31–32). Representing him vividly as a lusty, crude 'bruiser', Winterson describes how according to myth his foster-mother the goddess Hera was deceived into suckling him as a baby and thereby giving him immortality. In revenge Hera tries to drive him mad, which leads to the killing of six of his own children at which point he goes to Delphy to ask forgiveness and is ordered to perform the 12 famous labours. The novella picks up Heracles's story at the point where he is performing number 11 – to procure the golden apples from Hera's tree in the garden of the Hesperides, which Atlas tended before he was punished. Heracles asks Atlas for help procuring the apples and offers to take the weight of the world in return. Up to this point, Heracles has been a man of action, not given to contemplation, having spent 'twelve years clobbering snakes and thieving fruit' (p. 49), but Winterson's Heracles develops a degree of introspection and for the first time begins to question who he is: 'Why was he fixed, immoveable, plodding out his life like a magnificent ox?' (p. 45). When he encounters Atlas shouldering his unbearable burden, he asks the paradigm-shifting question: 'Why are we doing this mate?' (p. 49). Defeated by the gods, Atlas argues that 'that there is no such thing as freedom'; 'there is only the will of the god's and man's fate' (p. 51). Winterson therefore pits the classical world view of a divinely ordained destiny against the modern Enlightenment concept of self-determination in order to question both perspectives.

When Heracles takes the world on his shoulders, he cannot endure 'the slowly turning solitude'. The thought strikes him: 'What if Atlas never came back?' (p. 61). This new-found consciousness is represented as a 'thought wasp' buzzing around his head. Meanwhile Atlas picks apples, and finds that while the first and second apples are light, the third is too heavy to lift. The image develops the postmodern motif of relative values used throughout Winterson's fiction. An apple may represent 'a little world complete unto itself' (p. 66) and the world itself may be shouldered by a man. For the first time, Atlas begins 'to think that he had colluded in his punishment' by refusing to accept the boundaries of his life (p. 70). Hera appears to Atlas and tells him that the first two apples represent his past and future and the third is the present, 'made from your past, pointing towards your future' (p. 72). She offers to help him make a choice, but Atlas still believes that 'There is no choice. There is fate. No man escapes his fate' (p. 75). Hera tells him that he could have chosen differently and that he must now 'choose your destiny' (p. 76).

On Atlas's return Heracles tricks him into taking back the weight of the world. Heracles is ashamed of his act when he sees the grace and ease with which Atlas resumes his burden, but knows he will never return. Atlas, for his part, 'wanted to hurl the universe at Heracles, crush him, annihilate time' and, echoing a familiar Wintersonian refrain, 'make the story start again' (p. 83). Heracles makes some reparation for cheating Atlas by freeing Prometheus from his terrible punishment: chained to a rock, he is condemned to have a bird of prey tear out his liver every day for eternity. Yet, Heracles's own end is near; Hera's prophecy – 'No man shall kill Heracles, but a dead enemy' (p. 118) – comes true and he dies a terrible death by poisonous charm.

Winterson's treatment of Atlas's story, however, extends beyond the period designated by Greek myth into the present moment. Still shouldering the world, Atlas observes the disappearance of the gods and the coming of Christ: 'Time had become meaningless to Atlas. He was in a Black hole. He was under the event horizon' (p. 123). Atlas's fantastic existence in space-time is compared by Winterson to the relative value of time in space: 'In this vast city no two clocks kept the same time . . . While Mercury flew round the sun in days, Saturn took nearly twenty-one years' (p. 124). For Atlas, 'forever and never had become the same thing'

(p. 123). One day, Atlas sees a little face in a window of a space ship buzzing around his head; it is Laika, the dog sent into space by the Russians in 1957. Atlas frees her and she climbs up to sleep in the hollow of his shoulder:

> Atlas had long ago ceased to feel the weight of the world he carried, but he felt the skin and bone of this little dog. Now he was carrying something he wanted to keep, and that changed everything.
>
> (p. 127)

Responsibility born of love enters Atlas's world, just as did for Pew and Silver in *Lighthousekeeping*.

As in previous works, the novella contains autobiographical sections or interludes, which both rework aspects of Winterson's experience and provide a rationale for the novel. In a chapter entitled 'Leaning on the limits of myself', Winterson as author-narrator makes explicit her identification with Atlas's sense of loneliness and his desire to transcend the boundaries of his world. In a poignant version of her own 'origin story', which echoes *The PowerBook*, she makes the connection between herself and the Atlas myth:

> When I was born my mother gave me away to a stranger. I had no say in that. It was her decision, my fate. Later, my adopted mother rejected me too. And told me I was none of her, which was true. Having no one to carry me, I learned to carry myself. My girlfriend says I have an Atlas complex.
>
> (p. 97)

Just like Atlas, Winterson tells us, 'I can lift my own weight', but unlike the Titan, Winterson 'stayed on the run' (p. 98); like *The PowerBook*'s Ali, she apparently escapes her 'fate' by eluding fixed identity. Yet both she and her character experience the burden of living as intolerable. In a significant move away from postmodern 'ludism,'[5] the text works towards an understanding that the past cannot be ignored or wished away: 'I realise now that the past does not dissolve like a mirage. I realise that the future, though invisible, has weight. We are in the gravitational pull of the past and future' (p. 99). The text acknowledges the 'weight' of history, culture and habit in determining our lives – 'How many of us ever get free of our orbit?' (p. 99) – and interprets the ancients' belief in fate as a recognition of 'how hard it is for anyone to change anything' (p. 99). And yet, the text's response to the impossible burden is a familiar one: 'I want to tell the story again' (p. 100). Using myth, Winterson once more textualizes the problem of her own and human identity, and states, 'I chose this story above all others because it's a story I'm struggling to end' (p. 137). This suggests that the earlier *PowerBook*, while representing an end to the first seven-book cycle, does not resolve this particular issue. Indeed, Winterson insists, as she does throughout her work, 'I find there is no resolution' (p. 137).

Nevertheless, the resolution of *this* story comes as a revelation: 'Then Atlas had a strange thought. Why not put it down?' (p. 134). As Atlas lets his hands go from the sides of the world, the text clarifies the difference between a deterministic universe governed by mythological fate or mechanistic science and a (postmodern) decentred world of relativity and contingency: 'There was no burden. There was only the diamond-blue earth garnered in a wilderness of space' (p. 150). Ultimately, the novella affirms not Atlas's freedom from responsibility – because he commits himself to the care of the dog Laika – but freedom from himself. As Keulks (2007) argues, the novella presents a revisionist mythos of love and selfhood, in which Atlas ultimately aligns himself not with *The PowerBook*'s Ali, but with *Lighthousekeeping*'s Silver, choosing belonging over exile. And even the concluding image of Atlas and Laika walking away is similar to the final image of Pew and DogJim rowing away from the lighthouse. It is interesting that in her next novel, *The Stone Gods* (2007), in part a work of science fiction, Winterson chooses to pick up on the space theme explored here. Nevertheless, the wider question of where Winterson takes her writing from this point forward is a fascinating – and still very much open – one.

Part III
CRITICISM AND CONTEXTS

6

AUTHOR INTERVIEW

Your life is well documented, as is its interesting and dynamic relationship to your work. What in your childhood and early experience most shaped your adult life and outlook? And how would you characterize the ongoing relationship between your life and work, especially since becoming a well-known public figure?

The last line of *The Stone Gods* is 'Everything is imprinted forever with what it once was.' I don't believe we need be in thrall to the past, though many people are, and without even knowing it – it's the basis of Greek drama, but I do believe that the past is the territory we have to work with if we want to develop as human beings. Art began as a memory-system. Before we knew how to write, the oral tradition allowed important events to be preserved. Poetry, painting and carving were ways of keeping continuity with the past. Weirdly now, in our CCTV world, where everything is documented, we are in danger of losing continuity with the past. Art always puts its weight on the side of the imbalance, and so art has an important part to play now in helping us all to remember what it means to be human. We are in great danger of forgetting ourselves as human beings as science and the machine claim to do everything for us.

I do not want to pinpoint bits of my own life – my life works as a whole or not at all. Anyway, biography is at best entertaining, at worst misleading. It is also a way of avoiding real engagement with the work itself. Much easier to think about the life . . . What I do know is that if I stop developing as a human being, if I become fixed, set, closed, then whatever I write will be worthless.

While you yourself have situated your work in a European modernist tradition, your work has been variously described as postmodernist metafiction, and magical or fantastical realism. Are you comfortable with these epithets and do you feel part of a postmodernist movement in literature in the sense of the novel 'after' modernism? To what extent did you and do you see yourself as a specifically contemporary and experimental British writer alongside figures such as Angela Carter and Martin Amis?

Labels always strangle the scope of the work. I don't like, but don't really care about the labels, because all I want to do is get on with the work itself. What someone calls it is meaningless to me. It's as though you have your own name and when you go out in the street people start calling you by all sorts of other names, and then they get surprised or offended when you don't answer.

Literature is there for pleasure and for challenge. I worry that we tie people up in theory so that they lose touch with the excitement of reading. The writers who interest me most, right now, are Ali Smith and David Mitchell. I have always been a fan of Martin Amis, and we all know the huge contribution that Angela Carter has made to fiction. It's very good to have writers as friends, but very bad for writers, any writers, to play the academic game and start thinking of themselves in terms of 'movements' or 'groups'. Too much self-consciousness of that kind kills the energy of the work.

You famously wrote that there is no such thing as autobiography, only art and lies. Yet, despite your comments about the instability of identity, one has the sense reading your work as a whole that there is a distinct 'Wintersonian' persona whose voice and presence are felt across the range of your works. Is this a fair comment and how do you account for the simultaneously fragmented and persistent sense of (authorial) identity presented in your work?

I have never said that there is no such thing as identity – I'm with Jung that the whole of life is about the process of individuation – that is, bringing the conscious and unconscious parts of the self into relationship. No writer can live in the ego, daylight, rational self alone. We all work in liminal territory. If you can't read a page of mine and know that it is me, then I have failed, because a writer has to have a distinctive language. This is 'voice' not 'style'. We know who it is when we listen to Bach or Bowie. We know that Jackson Pollock is not Andy Warhol. The distinctiveness is there because the energized artist, in whatever medium, is colliding the raw material (in my case language) with a particular and highly personal sensibility. That pushes language itself into new territory, and it also pushes the writer into new territory. There is a constant back and forth between idea and expression. A common mistake is to assume that the writer has an idea and finds a language to express it. This is the case in non-fiction and journalism and works very well. It is not the case with creative work. There is a symbiosis and it is this symbiosis that is distinctive.

What I very much dislike is the current emphasis on celebrity and personality. I seem to have something of a magnetic personality for the press, and I honestly do not know why this is the case – I'm not being disingenuous here, but it bores me rigid. Judge me on my work, not on my shopping habits, not on my sex life, not on my house in the country . . .

Your wide reading of the Western literary canon and your interest in post-Enlightenment science are evident in your work. Your writing also appears to share concerns with contemporary philosophy such as the work of Judith Butler and Julia Kristeva. Is this the case and in what ways does contemporary thought inform your work?

I am interested in anything, everything, a long as it is real. I don't see how anyone can be a writer or want to be a writer if they don't read as widely, or as deeply, as they can. I am astonished and disturbed to find how little reading is encouraged in many schools and universities. The new thing of just reading part of a text is insanity. Who are the salaried civil servants who dictate this rubbish and why does any teacher or academic go along with it? I want life, and as much of it as I can get, that means experience, yes, but it also means testing experience against ideas, against dreams, against poetry, against science. The best of life is like bumper cars at the fairground – you collide all the time, it's not a crash, but the collision should affect the way you go round the circuit next time. My mind is constantly colliding with other minds. That's exciting.

How far do you acknowledge the importance of a lesbian literary tradition, particularly Woolf's work, to your own writing? Notwithstanding its universal interests, does your work address lesbian readers and women readers in particular ways? How do you see the relationship between the universal and the particular in your work?

I am sure I didn't call Woolf a 'lesbian writer': a) she isn't one; b) she would hate the label; c) I hate the label. Nothing is more boring than wrapping your whole self around your sexuality. I am not interested in that. We write, and either we write well, or we don't. The end.

Of course there is stuff written especially for a gay or lesbian audience, no problem with that, but I don't want to read it and I don't want to write it. I have made this completely clear in my essay 'The Semiotics of Sex' (in *Art Objects*). The sexuality of a writer is not the business of literary criticism; to make it so is a cheap way out of dealing with the work on its terms and in its own right. *Oranges* is not a 'gay' book, and neither is anything else that I have written. I will always stand up for tolerance and honesty, I really won't stand up for all this PC sexual politics stuff which buries the energy of the work under the incredibly dull and simple-minded concerns of queer theory.

You refer to your first seven books from Oranges to The PowerBook as a complete cycle. Are there any emerging characteristics of your second cycle which includes Lighthousekeeping, Weight and The Stone Gods?

I can't answer this; I am inside my work not outside it.

Some readers of your recent work detected something of a rapprochement with literary realism in terms of historical grounding, characterization and storytelling. Is this a fair assessment in your view?

Again, don't know, don't care, the taxonomy means nothing to me, I want to do the work I do in the way I am driven to do it, at the time of doing it. *To write* is an active verb. The doing is everything.

Your work extends well beyond the literary text to encompass journalism, work for the stage and screen, broadcasting, a strong web presence and other non-fiction works of various kinds. How important to you are these compared to the writing of fiction and how do you see the relationship between these different media? Are they all different means of achieving the same thing or something quite distinct from each other?

I have always felt as though I run something like an artisan's workshop, and I can make a chair or a table, a wooden bowl or a set of shelves, or a cabinet with secret drawers. I am a writer – therefore I can write, and how that takes shape is really not the main question. Creative work takes huge energy, and asks for something that cannot be learned, whatever the people coining money on the creative writing courses tell you. For me, as long as I can write fiction, I can write anything. When I am not able anymore to write fiction, I will be just a professional, or a jobber, and the lit-up place won't be there. The lit-up place is what makes the other work glitter a bit. The reason people want me to do journalism is that I can make it glitter a bit, but that is because of the creative work that lends its light elsewhere.

As for stage and screen, they are challenging, but again, they depend on what is central to me – the fiction. As for the website, well, this is the world we live in. Gotta have a website, and therefore, gotta have a good one where people feel I am trying for them. That's why I have the Message Board and why I write the monthly column.

My concerns have always been the same: to stretch the possibilities of fiction and to work with language so that it is metaphor as well as meaning. I want words to double and tilt, I want them to shift matter – heavy solid matter, with a lightness that is possible because language itself is light – both not weighed down, and illuminating. All I do is work with what is there – language is there – we are in danger of losing its power along with our own power as human beings. I want kids to find the words and to be part of that discovery.

Communication? Yes, always, but not at any price.

You have written two works for children to date. Are there any similarities – in style, theme and approach – between these and your work for adults, or are they distinct? What is your view of contemporary children's fiction?

Like I said I don't do lit crit on my own work. The only thing to do with a writer is read her or him. I reckon that if anyone wants to make the comparison between what I do for kids and not for kids, they had better start reading and then make up their own minds.

I write for kids now because I have two godchildren and I want to entertain them. Some godmothers can knit, others can tell stories. But I am sure that if kids learn to love books early, it stays with them. I was always a supporter of *Harry Potter*. I've read them all, the godchildren have read them all. Of course I prefer the Pullman trilogy, but interestingly, the kids don't. The elder one knows it is 'better' but she doesn't love it. *Harry Potter* made a connection.

Your interest in everything from modern art to contemporary British life and manners is evident from your journalism and non-fiction writing. What in your view is the role of the intellectual as opposed to the celebrity in contemporary culture and how do you see your own role as a public figure?

It is very important to speak up and speak out for what you believe. A writer should speak out – and I very much dislike the cynicism and moral emptiness of those media types who savage any writer who wants to speak seriously and honestly about our world. Martin Amis was heavily criticized for his essays *The Second Plane*. There is no need to agree with all he says, or indeed any of what he says, but to suggest that he shouldn't say it, is disturbing.

For myself, I am glad to use any platform offered to me if I can influence thinking or stimulate debate. Cynicism is death. We didn't become cynical as a society until the 1980s. It's not cool to be cynical, it's cynical to be cynical. Give it up! Work for change!

I don't want to be a personality or a mini-celeb, I am a writer. A writer, an artist, is a practical person; we make things. I work to make things happen.

Can you describe your new novel, The Stone Gods? What led you to utilize the science fiction genre? What will your next publication (after the children's book) be about? What other projects are you working on and how do you see your work developing in the next few years?

If every book set in the future is science fiction then every book set in the past, even yesterday, is a historical novel. More labels . . . I can't describe *The Stone Gods*, it was all I could do to write it. My work there is done, and now, if anyone wants to know what it is, well, they'll just have to read it. No short cuts, no cribs, no way out but through.

What I can say is that the novel asks what might happen if we were to discover a new planet fit for life. I use both Nietzsche and Ouspensky and the idea of eternal return – not in the Buddhist sense, but in the sense of endlessly making the same mistakes. The novel also asks what might happen if the UK were subject to serious attack – my view is that government would fail and this would be a perfect opportunity for corporate interests to take over. But it isn't a depressing book. It is a book about the individual inside the mass, and what we do with our individuality, if we have any to do anything with . . .

I never know what I will write next. Just because you have written a book, or ten, or twenty, doesn't mean that you can ever, will ever, write another one. You could copy yourself, or others, but that would be cheating.

Art, in all its forms, is the one place where lying never ever brings any advantage. Art is a place where we have to tell the truth. And where we should respond truthfully. There is not one truth, there is not one response, but to avoid the work, by substituting biography or gossip, theory or politics, is a form of lying – we lie to ourselves and we lie about the piece of work. It is better to meet the shining place straight on. That obtains for the making of it too. If what you are doing is real it will challenge everything. If the work you are doing, as a writer, doesn't challenge everything – the everything you are at the time of making – all your skill, all your knowledge, all your assumptions, all your success, if all of that is not back in the balance, then you are not risking yourself. Books have a way of finding us out.

7

OTHER WRITING

In addition to her 11 novels, Winterson has produced a wide range of other writing including short stories, essays on art and culture, children's fiction, adaptations for the stage and the screen, original play-scripts, journalism, and writing for her website jeanettewinterson.com. In fact, the only genre she has not attempted would appear to be poetry. Given that her work is often described by critics and by Winterson herself as intensely 'poetic', this may seem surprising. Winterson explains this apparent anomaly by admitting that 'Poetry is the thing that matters to me more than anything else. [. . .] But I don't write it because I have decided that my experiment is to use those poetic disciplines and work them against the stretchiness of narrative' (Winterson, 2005, p. 10). As she states, it is words that matter most to Winterson and it is her love of language that she seeks to communicate whatever medium she happens to be working in.

SHORT STORIES

In addition to pieces of original short fiction that have appeared in the broadsheet press such as the *Guardian* Christmas Stories,[1] Winterson has published a collection of short stories, *The World and Other Places* (1998). The stories crystallize many of the themes explored at greater length in her novels including the nature of desire, the quest for meaning, the power of the imagination and the constraints of (gender) identity. Moving easily between female and male narrators, and encompassing a range of literary styles, the stories blend elements of the magical and the real. In the title story, which retells the myth of Icarus, a boy dreams of being a pilot and grows up to fly solo 'into the end stream of the sun'

(*WP*, p. 100). His humble, working-class family understands the power of the imagination to transport the self from humdrum surroundings to a magical realm; they play a 'flying game' where they each imagine they are on an aeroplane trip. The childhood game fires the boy's ambition – 'I was waiting to invent myself' (p. 92). As a man, he joins the Air Force and travels to the places he dreamt about, but something is missing and he begins to consider the question of how to live. The qualities of 'adventure, manliness, action' (p. 98) that had defined him now seem lacking and he pilots his own plane around the world in search of personal meaning. The story picks up on a central Wintersonian motif, that of self-invention through the journey or quest. The story ends with the airman flying his plane back to his parents' house and, to the astonishment of the neighbours, taking to the skies once more in a euphoric gesture of freedom.

In 'The poetics of sex', Sappho, the first-person narrator, describes her relationship with her female lover, Picasso, under headings which demonstrate the crass and prurient attitude of mainstream culture to lesbian couples: 'Why do you sleep with girls?'; 'Which one of you is the man?'; and the infamous 'What do lesbians do in bed?'. As the story unfolds, Winterson confounds the assumptions behind such questions by thoroughly blurring the boundaries between masculine and feminine roles and referents. In the continuous interchange of sexual roles, identity becomes performative rather than fixed: 'Whose on top depends on where you're standing but as we're lying down it doesn't matter' (p. 35). To the question 'were you born a lesbian?', the narrator replies, 'I could say yes, I could say no, . . . both statements would be true' (p. 36), thereby refusing to fix the 'truth' of sexual identity in a similar manner to that advocated by Butler (2004) as a means of 'troubling' gender. However, the narrator goes on to insist that 'lesbians are true, at least to one another, if not to the world' (*WP*, p. 36).

In many ways the story is a companion piece to Winterson's earlier novel *Art & Lies*, which also contains 'characters' called Sappho and Picasso and undertakes a similar experiment with both sexual identity and language. As in the novel, Winterson's language in the short story is dense, poetic and sensual, utilizing striking conceits and a strong form of alliteration to create its effects: 'She rushes for me bull-subtle, butching at the gate as if she's come to stud' (*WP*, p. 31). As in this example, Winterson plays with butch and femme signifiers in a manner reminiscent of Djuna Barnes' *Nightwood* and Gertrude Stein's prose-poetry, both of which use modernist techniques of defamiliarization and intertextual punning to push at the boundaries of sexual discourse. In another example – 'Beneath the sheets we practice Montparnasse' (p. 34) – Winterson appears to reference both lesbian sexual practice and the 'women of the Left Bank' who took up residence in Paris in the early years of the twentieth century (Benstock, 1986). Like Djuna Barnes, Winterson makes use of animal symbolism as well as mixing sacred and profane imagery to striking effect, describing Picasso as a Madonna who performs miracles 'of the physical kind' (*WP*, p. 33). And like Barnes, Winterson uses the grotesque and the abject in order, paradoxically, to celebrate lesbian love.

The story is called 'The *poetics* of sex' (my emphasis), but it also explores the *politics* of sex. It demonstrates very clearly Winterson's desire to make an ideological as well as a literary intervention in the writing of sex, to appropriate and transform language so it speaks for all subjects, including, especially, women. As the narrator states, 'When I see a word held hostage to manhood I have to rescue it' (p. 39). This story is also among Winterson's most explicit and powerful critiques of homophobia and heterosexism:

> The world is full of blind people. They don't see Picasso and me dignified by our love. They see perverts, inverts, tribades, homosexuals. They see circus freaks and Satan worshippers, girl-catchers and porno turn-ons. Picasso says they don't know how to look at pictures either.
>
> (p. 37)

The lovers retreat to Sappho's island, Lesbos, a female space where, in contrast to the heterosexual mainland, women are free to work and love. Implicitly invoking the French feminist visions of Cixous and Irigaray, the narrator declares, 'we have found the infinite variety of woman' (p. 41). The story ends with the narrator, Sappho, describing Picasso's painting, adding 'and I have written this' (p. 45) in a self-reflexive acknowledgement of the writing process. Taken as a whole, this collection of stories is of interest to students of Winterson's work, not only for the way it treats in miniature themes she develops in the novels but also for its lack of inhibition, especially regarding lesbian themes.

In another story with an island theme, 'Turn of the World', Winterson develops the metaphor of fiction as travel to ruminate on the nature of storytelling. The four islands – Fyr, Hydor, Areos and Erde – represent the elements. Aeros, as its name suggests, is an air-born island, 'not be found in the same place for a week together' (p. 158). Reminiscent of the magical cities in *Sexing the Cherry*, it defies both gravity and logic and enables flights of the imagination: 'The people of Aeros are great storytellers' and 'the only way to travel is by story' (p. 159). Deep in the heart of the island lies a forest which, Winterson suggests, is the source of all the stories in the world:

> Anyone who sits for long enough and narrows his eyes on the strip of forest he can penetrate will see strange shapes moving in half light. Is that Hercules in a lion skin? Is that Icarus waxed into gold wings? Is that Siegfried's horn in the distance? Is that Lancelot's horse?
>
> (p. 160)

The references to Greek myth, folk tale and Grail legend echo throughout Winterson's work and as Peter Childs observes, 'This seems to intimate how the forest of fairy tales, so prominent in Winterson's books from *Oranges* to *The PowerBook*, is the primal home of all stories, which spin off or spiral in their own directions but remain variations on a few themes' (2005, p. 264).

ESSAYS

Winterson has published a collection of essays on art and literature, the punningly titled *Art Objects: Essays on Ecstasy and Effrontery* (1995), in which 'objects' works as both noun and verb. Although not taken very seriously by critics (Lambert, 1998), the essays show Winterson as a self-consciously modernist writer, with a knowledgeable interest in aesthetic theory. Written in response to the criticism of her novel *Art & Lies*, the book contains a spirited defence of her own uncompromisingly intense poetic style. The topics range from a discussion of how to read works of art to a celebration of the genius of Virginia Woolf, whose writing permeates the essays. Part I describes the genesis and growth of Winterson's love of modern art, recounting how she learnt to understand and appreciate its difficulty and foreignness using the art critic Roger Fry as her guide. 'Art takes time', she tells us (*AO*, p. 7), contrasting it favourably with the instantaneous and disposable character of popular culture.

Part II, 'Transformations', consists of four essays on literary aesthetics: a general essay on the modernist challenge to realism; an essay discussing Stein as a key modernist; and two essays celebrating Woolf's radical writing practice in *Orlando* and *The Waves*. The essay on Stein provides an interesting analysis of the furore that surrounded the 1934 publication of *The Autobiography of Alice B. Toklas*. Fellow writers and artists, many of whom featured as characters in the book, were highly critical of the work's 'inaccuracy'. Winterson points out the irony of modernist artists condemning Stein in the name of realism, thereby assuming that 'autobiography is a rigid mould into which facts must be poured' (*AO*, p. 47). By fictionalizing the people around her, Stein questions the veracity of 'identity' and performs a deconstruction of the autobiography genre:

> *The Autobiography of Alice B. Toklas* is not Gertrude ghosting Alice, it is Gertrude refusing to accept that real people need to be treated really. She included herself. Gertrude Stein made all of the people around her into characters in her own fiction. I think that a splendid blow to verisimo and one which simultaneously questions identity, the nature of truth and the purpose of art.
>
> (p. 51)

In a similar way, Woolf deconstructed the biography genre in *Orlando*, smuggling in the 'contraband' subjects of lesbianism and feminism. Winterson particularly admires *Orlando* for its stretching of imaginative limits and for the way it crosses borders of both genre and gender. She places herself with Woolf and Stein as experimenters and debunkers of literary genre. 'Woolf can gallop English', she writes, comparing her to the mythical horse Pegasus in an allusion to her favourite metaphor of flight: 'Virginia Woolf has the gift of wings' (p. 77).

Part III contains essays on the pleasures of book collecting, a celebration of art as imagination and an exploration of the relation between the author's art and life. In the most well-known essay 'The semiotics of sex', Winterson intervenes in the debate about the relationship between an author's sexuality and their work, 'writing back' to the public world in which her work is constructed. She argues strongly against what she calls the 'sexualization' of art, accusing academic queer theorists as much as mainstream culture of narrowing the scope and reach of her work. Rejecting the label 'lesbian writer', she makes the key point that 'Art is difference, but not necessarily sexual difference' (p. 104). She adds that 'If queer culture is now working against assumptions of identity as sexuality, art gets their first' (p. 106). For Winterson, though, art must always take precedence over politics: Eliot is a better writer than Stephen Spender, if less of a sex radical. And she insists, 'When I read Rich or Wilde . . . their homosexuality is less important than their art' (p. 109). As her fiction also demonstrates, it is the universal rather than the particular experience that she values in art, or, as she puts it, 'the shared human connection that traces the past and the future in the whorl of now' (p. 117).

The book contains two main aesthetic ideas: first, that art and literature should be 'difficult' and challenge the reader; and secondly, that art exists in a distinct realm and should be seen as a re-making of the world rather than a reflection of it. Both these ideas are heavily indebted to the theories expounded by modernist writers such as Virginia Woolf in *A Room of One's Own* and T.S. Eliot in his essay 'Tradition and the Individual Talent', which, at times, Winterson echoes almost verbatim:

> [. . .] the calling of the artist, in any medium is to make it new. I do not mean that in new work the past is repudiated; quite the opposite, the past is reclaimed. It is not lost to authority, it is not absorbed at a level of familiarity. It is restated and re-instated in its original vigour.
>
> (AO, p. 12)

While Winterson generally provides a compelling defence of 'art for art's sake', at times, the argument falters. For example, having argued that 'art cannot be tamed', she then concedes that once shocking works – such as Constable's landscapes – can become domesticated and conventional. As elsewhere in her writing – and, it could be argued, in Woolf's – the (modernist) transcendental view of art is at odds with a more materialist social constructionist viewpoint. For students of her work, the collection is indispensable for an understanding of how she regards her own aesthetic practice and position in relation to literary tradition.

CHILDREN'S FICTION

Winterson has written two books for children to date: the picture book *The King of Capri* (2003); and a novel for older children, *Tanglewreck* (2006). A fairy tale with a gentle moral about sharing with others, *The King of Capri* tells the story of a greedy and selfish king who wishes he had more mouths to eat all the food he desires and never thinks about the people who barely have enough food to fill one mouth. One night a great tempest blows all the king's clothes over the Bay of Naples to the house of a washerwoman named Mrs Jewel. In true fairy tale style, each experiences a reversal of fortune so Mrs Jewel becomes the Queen of Naples and the now impoverished King is left to repent his former profligacy. Where the King was greedy and selfish, Mrs Jewel is modest and generous. The King rows across the bay to find this new Queen, and comes to realize what Mrs Jewel has that he had lacked:

> The King was silent for a while and, while he was silent, he was looking at the sunshine and the flowers and wondering why he never used to look at them before. Then he looked at Mrs Jewel and thought she was as lovely as sunshine and flowers and that if she were with him he would be happy and good for the rest of his life.
>
> (*KC*, p. 24)

Of course, the King asks Mrs Jewel to marry him; of course, she says 'yes' and they live happily ever after. Despite its fantastic character, the story is filled with workaday details about eating and doing the laundry, which are reportedly two of Winterson's favourite pastimes (*Saturday Live* Interview). The text is accompanied by attractive illustrations by Jane Ray using appropriately jewel-like colours.

Winterson's first full-length novel for children, *Tanglewreck*, is a fantasy adventure story about a magical clock called the Timekeeper, which also features some wonderfully gothic houses, imaginary creatures and thrilling pursuits through time and space. Its heroine is Silver, an orphan girl who lives in a Tudor house called *Tanglewreck* and is entrusted with the task of finding the Timekeeper and thus restoring Time itself which has been hijacked by an evil consortium led by the villainous Regalia Mason. As well as introducing children to Quantum Physics and the Theory of Relativity, the novel carries a moral message about the speed and wastefulness of modern life, warning that 'we are using up Time too fast, just as we are using up all the other resources of the Earth' (p. 126).

The novel is clearly partly inspired by Philip Pullman's *His Dark Materials*, which Winterson is known to admire (*Times*, 2007). While very much her own (Wintersonian) heroine, Silver is similar to Pullman's feisty heroine Lyra; whereas Winterson's villainous characters Abel Darkwater and Regalia Mason bear a strong resemblance to Pullman's Lord Asriel and Mrs Coulter respectively. Both writers provide powerful and seductive female villains, and Regalia Mason is more than a match for Pullman's Mrs Coulter. Also known as Maria Prophetessa, Regalia Mason is a wonderful creation, a seemingly ageless alchemist who moves effortlessly with the times, replacing her crystal ball with a Sat Nav system, and running Quanta, a global business which sells Time. As she states, 'Science had done away with so much magic and mumbo-jumbo' (*T*, p. 203). Winterson's Abel Darkwater is perhaps a more one-dimensional version of Lord Asriel, but, in an intertextual nod to Winterson's own work, shares part of his name with a character from her adult novel *Lighthousekeeping*. Instead of Pullman's alethiometer, which detects dust, Winterson has the Timekeeper, an ancient and magical object with the power to regulate Time. The novel also involves a plot similar to Pullman's, and indeed to numerous other fantasy adventure stories: the plot to control the universe. 'Whoever controls Time controls the universe' (p. 86), Abel repeatedly states. Arguably, the atomizing process at the heart of Winterson's plot actually makes more sense than Pullman's somewhat obscure dust idea.

As Winterson comments, the test of good children's fantasy is the creation of an alternative imaginative universe which nevertheless is absolutely believable (*Times*, 2007). *Tanglewreck* more than meets this criterion, creating a range of fantasy *nova* which fire the imagination. These include the woolly mammoth Goliath, preserved in the ice after the Great Frost and living in the culverts on the banks of the Thames; and the Throwbacks, a group of troglodytic folk who escaped from Bedlam hospital in the eighteenth century and ride about the underground on 'petrol ponies', their name for 1930s Enfield motorbikes. Among her striking invented features are the Time tornadoes – 'strange disruptions in the fabric of time' (p. 28) – into which people disappear only to be thrown up somewhere else in time. Above all, *Tanglewreck* underscores the importance of adventure to children. As in all successful epic narratives for children (just as for adults), such as *Lord of the Rings*, which has inspired J.K Rowling as well as Winterson and Pullman, there is a quest at the novel's heart, which the hero or heroine must agree to perform. Frodo Baggins, Harry Potter, Lyra and Silver must all *choose* to go on their perilous missions, in the process learning the lessons of life, acquiring self-reliance and self-knowledge as well as worldly wisdom.

Another of Winterson's inspired inventions is the Einstein Line, an interstellar crossroads where Time is steady, and Checkpoint Zero, which polices the boundary between past, present and future. In an obvious reference to immigration control, 'Blow-ins' arrive on a daily basis only to be deported back to their own time. Through such invented features, the novel provides children with an accessible and delightful introduction to science including Einstein's Theory of Relativity and Quantum Physics. As in her previous novels, Winterson represents the world not as a collection of solid objects, but in terms of the dynamic transfer of energy and information. Her relativist philosophy, familiar from her adult novels, runs throughout the text: 'Nothing is solid, nothing is fixed. The future forks with new beginnings and different ends' (*T*, p. 410); 'Every possibility is always present, though only one outcome is chosen' (p. 214). Winterson thus exploits the implications of the Theory of Relativity to the full, working it in to the plot to manipulate and control Time.

According to Kate Kellaway '*Tanglewreck* is a full-blooded return to form. It is ambitious, entertaining and metaphysical [...] and it is the freshest, most energetic novel she has written in years' (Kellaway, 2006). As Kellaway comments, the novel not only tells an entrancing story but gives full rein to Winterson's sense of humour, her imagination and her inner child (*ibid.*). As explored elsewhere in the study, as a writer Winterson identifies strongly with the figure of the child, and some of her best work is written from the child's simultaneously 'innocent' and knowing perspective. This is a view echoed by Geraldine Bedell in her review for the *Guardian*: 'Writing for children seems to have lent warmth to Winterson's voice and the novel is leavened with a kind, godmotherly assurance that makes it not merely impressive but enormously likable, and fun' (Bedell, 2006).

ORIGINAL WORK FOR TV, FILM AND RADIO

Although predominantly known as a novelist, Winterson began writing for other media very early on in her writing career. In 1988 she wrote her first radio play for BBC Radio 3: called *Static*, it was the story of a Lancashire housewife, May, who becomes fascinated with an old radio her husband has discovered in the process of redecorating. In the same year, inspired by conversations with a friend, the television producer and actress Vicky Licorish, about her mother's life, Winterson wrote a short film called *Great Moments in Aviation* (dir. Paul Shearer). A few years later, Winterson reworked the script with the same BBC team of Bibon Kidron and Philippa Giles responsible for *Oranges*. Renamed *Shades of Fear* and starring Vanessa Redgrave and Jonathan Pryce, the film was premiered at the Cannes Film Festival in 1993 and was broadcast by the BBC in November 1995. The plot concerns a young black woman from the Caribbean, Gabriel Angel, who travels from Grenada to England in the early 1950s to become an aviator. The film treats some familiar Wintersonian themes: love, freedom, identity as masquerade, and the politics of gender, race and class. The characters embark on a long transatlantic journey but are never seen disembarking on arrival in England. According to Winterson, what is important is not the identity or destination of the characters, but the journey, both literal and psychological, they undertake. However, it was not a great success and, in the introduction to the script, Winterson commented, 'I do not feel, as I did with the TV version of *Oranges Are Not the Only Fruit*, that *Great Moments in Aviation* is the definitive film. I could not see how we could have done Oranges better, I do see how we could have done Great Moments better' (Winterson, 1994, p. xii).

Winterson resumed playwriting in 2001 and a new play, *Text Message*, was broadcast on BBC Radio 3. The play explored the relationship between technology and writing practices, a subject that she had already treated in *The PowerBook* (2000). In 2002 Winterson wrote a television documentary for the BBC exploring the genesis and impact of Virginia Woolf's *Orlando*. In 2005, Winterson collaborated with the cellist Natalie Clein on a performance piece based on Bach's *Goldberg Variations* in which music and text intertwine. Lucasta Miller observed that 'the text sounds rather Eliot-like: impressionistic, rather like a poem, architectural, formally shaped, with hard, clear images, no characters, just a voice' (Miller, 2005, p. 11). It is fitting then that Fiona Shaw, who appeared in a solo performance of Eliot's 'The Waste Land', was once again part of the cast when it was staged in Paris in October 2005.

ADAPTATIONS FOR STAGE AND SCREEN

In the introduction to the script of *Oranges*, Winterson states, 'My interest in working for film and television is inevitably evangelical' (Winterson, 1994, p. viii). For Winterson then, the business of adaptation, translating her own novels to the stage or screen, is about getting her message across to the greatest number in the widest number of forms. In addition, Winterson's adaptation work represents an example of intertextual exchange between different art forms in which rewriting becomes a dynamic and transformative practice, a process that interests Winterson for its own sake. Her first – and to date most successful – adapted work was the BBC television adaptation of *Oranges*, which was screened in January 1990 starring Charlotte Coleman as Jess and Geraldine McEwan as Mrs Winterson. The film was greeted with almost universal critical acclaim (see Hinds, 1992) and went on to win numerous awards including a BAFTA in the UK and the Prix Italia for the 'Best TV Drama' in 1991. It also raised Winterson's public profile considerably and led to increased sales of her novels; understandably, she professed herself very pleased with the result (Dunn, 1990).

Inevitably, a number of changes have been effected in the translation from page to screen. First, in the screen version, the protagonist is renamed Jess, which has the effect of distancing the role from the author herself. In other ways, Coleman perfectly embodies the fictional Wintersonian heroine: small, feisty and red headed (requiring Coleman to dye her hair). McEwan, too, arguably gives the performance of her life in a perfect rendition of the formidable and eccentric Mrs Winterson. The screen version is also a less obviously 'postmodern' text; indeed, Marshment and Hallam argue that the adaptation may be seen as a 'realist text' (1994, p. 146). While it is certainly the case that the adaptation has not translated onto the screen the novel's inset fairy tales and passages of philosophical musing, nevertheless it arguably incorporates the 'fantasy' aspects of the novel by other means. These include the carnivalesque and 'other-worldly' opening credit sequence with its eerie and discordant 'fairground' music, and the slightly surreal *mise-en-scène* which characterizes the whole film. Taken together, these techniques work to render Northern working-class life in terms of grotesque realism, taking it beyond the conventions of naturalistic TV drama, whether of the 'period' or kitchen sink variety.

A key difference lies in the representation of religious extremism; in the novel, although fanatical and oppressive, the members of Jeanette's church never inflict physical violence on her after she flouts Church teaching. Believing her to be possessed by the devil, they lock her in the house and wait for her to recant. In the screen version, the exorcism becomes a much more sinister and sadistic spectacle as Pastor Finch physically wrestles the demon out of Jess's body. In one scene, Kenneth Cranham's large frame is seen straddling Charlotte Coleman's frail body as she is held down. It is possible, I would argue, that such an extreme representation may function simultaneously in two contradictory ways: at a conscious level to win audience sympathy for the lesbian heroine, and at an unconscious level to punish her for that very sexual transgression.

The 'sex scenes' are another aspect where significant changes have taken place. In the novel, Winterson does not explicitly describe the young women's lovemaking, leaving it up to the reader's imagination. In the screen version, however, these scenes are inevitably given more prominence by being realized in a visual medium. It seems that Winterson was keen to take up the challenge of putting lesbian sex on screen: when writing the sex scene she commented that she wanted to create an encounter that 'wouldn't be dirty raincoats or like *Desert Hearts* where the women appeared to have no "hands"' (Winterson, 1990, p. 26). The resulting scene shows the young women embracing passionately and clearly having sex but, as critics have pointed out, it was carefully constructed to conform to BBC quality television standards of taste (Hinds, 1992); indeed the *Daily Mail* could not fault it. The criticism could be made that the extreme slenderness of the actresses allowed for a certain infantilization of the characters and their lovemaking, a strategy common to cultural representations of lesbianism. On the other hand, given that Jess and her lover are still girls – aged 15 – this representation is not inappropriate. Marchment and Hallam argue that the adaptation successfully 'naturalizes' lesbian sexuality within the conventions of 'young love' (1994, p. 150) and therefore works against the pathologization of homosexuality. Regardless of the nuances of these interpretations, it is undeniable that a milestone in the onscreen representation of lesbianism was reached. In one of the first and most sensitive analyses of the screen adaptation, Hilary Hinds notes the phenomenal and unprecedented success of Oranges in 'crossing over' from the margins to the mainstream of British culture. She attributes this, fascinatingly, to its lesbian features, which she argues enable it to move between boundaries of high and low, margins and mainstream:

> [. . .] Oranges as a complete cultural product – author, novel, television drama – seems consistently to elude and collapse these categories. Central to this elusiveness seems to be the text's lesbianism. Although it may be true to say that the lesbianism is diffused by the text's associations with high culture and its consequent openness to a liberal interpretation, it is also true to say that Oranges has retained, and increased, its lesbian audience and its subcultural consumption, and has also been praised by a tabloid press usually hostile to lesbian and gay issues.
>
> (Hinds, 1992, p. 170)

Unfortunately, Winterson's next adaptation project, the film adaptation of The Passion, did not go as planned. At the turn of the millennium Winterson was working on a screenplay for Miramax Films, supposed to star Gwyneth Paltrow and Juliette Binoche, but in 2000 Emma Brockes reported in the Guardian that the production company rejected Winterson's script as 'too long and complicated' (2000, p. 6).

Winterson's other major adaptation has been a theatre work based on her novel The PowerBook in a co-production by the National Theatre of London and the Théâtre National de Chaillot of Paris. The play was premiered in London on 18 May 2002 as part of the Lyttleton Transformation Project, and thereafter in

Paris between 17 and 27 September 2003, and at the RomaEuropa Festival in Rome between 3 and 5 October 2003. At first glance, *The PowerBook* is a less obvious choice for adaptation than *Oranges*, being a highly literary text that does not seem to lend itself to theatrical staging. However, the novel's exploration of computer technologies positions it as the product of a multimedia era and it is this aspect that the play foregrounds. Winterson devised the theatre work in collaboration with the director Deborah Warner and the actress Fiona Shaw, both of whom had experience of theatre versions of non-theatrical texts. When Warner first approached Winterson for the rights, she said she 'wanted to make a new kind of theatre' (Winterson, 2002). The challenge of 'making it new', the chance to work with Warner and Shaw and to renew her acquaintance with the theatre (she worked at The Roundhouse when she first came to London) all inspired Winterson. From the start she was clear that she did not want it to be a straightforward adaptation: using the image of a vase broken into a thousand pieces to describe the relationship between original and adaptation, she wanted to create something new, which would stand alone as a theatrical work (Winterson, 2003). In the programme notes, Winterson gives the following account of the work's genesis:

> *The Powerbook* experiment is to take text – much as Deborah and Fiona did in *The Waste Land*, and let the drama happen through it. The text becomes a prism through which light can be passed. As the light passes through it (invention, direction, acting, music, set, can be called the light here), shapes and shadows and colours appear, and some things are enlarged and others shrink away. The development of the form is organic – only at the last possible second do we fix it. Above all, we trust the text, and that is where we differ from a workshop or devised piece. There are formal boundaries – and we agreed at the start that if *The Powerbook* itself collapsed under the pressure, we would abandon the project.
>
> (Winterson, 2002)

Does the finished piece work as an adaptation and as drama? The play, like the novel, reworks some of the classics of Western literature including Boccaccio, Dante, Shakespeare, Marvell and Donne. As Winterson stated, this is not the death of the book; just a transformation of it into something else. As an adaptation, it necessarily dispenses with the highly self-referential, metafictional sections of the novel, focussing on the stories of the 'great and ruinous lovers' which are inset stories in the novel. This works well, drawing intertextual parallels between sexual politics in the past and present. The play concentrates on contrasting a modern-day couple with two tragic pairings from the past: Lancelot and Guinevere (from Arthurian legend) and Paolo and Francesca da Rimini (from a story by Boccaccio). The performance represented a celebration of love and the language of love in which the past is reanimated in the dialogue between the medieval and the contemporary scenes. The casting, too, was inspired with female actors playing both male and female roles in the tradition of theatrical cross-dressing and in keeping with the novel's gender-ambivalent hero/heroine Ali/Alix. Fiona Shaw doubles up to play both Lancelot and the doomed Francesca, capitalizing on her tall, masculine appearance and her reputation for playing male leads.[2] Saffron Burrows plays the beloved as an incarnation of the many love objects in Winterson's novels.

As theatre, it is clear that set designer Tom Pye and lighting designer Jean Kalman worked hard to produce a striking multi-media experience. Pye created special visual effects which transformed the theatre into the inside of a computer with the result that 'through projected images, the stage becomes a site of passage from the second to the third dimension' (Schifferes, 2002). But as drama, the adaptation is oddly static, failing to capture the narrative movement of the novel as the protagonist taps out her email narratives and pursues her online romance. It is more akin to a series of tableaux than modern drama, once more gesturing towards older artistic traditions.

Critical responses to the play were extremely mixed and reflect the tension between the elements of drama and the spectacle identified above. Paul Taylor, writing in *The Independent*, commented that the audience was faced with 'the spectacle of an actress [Shaw] stuck in a theatre piece whose cyberspace metaphor is quickly exposed as being more an embarrassing encumbrance than a genuine organising principle' and that the play failed to communicate 'the addictiveness of being online' (2002). In contrast, for Nicholas De Jongh the adaptation succeeded in capturing 'Winterson's rare, strange, lyric eloquence' (2002), while Michael Billington claimed that Winterson's work 'gains from the tangible physicality of the theatre and gleefully combines eroticism and wit' (2002). In the programme notes, Winterson makes it clear that she envisaged the work both as a journey and as a dialogue between the art of the past and the art of the present (2002), and for her, at least, the journey was a worthwhile one.[3]

JOURNALISM

Winterson has been writing for the broadsheet press for many years, with regular columns in *The Guardian* (2001–2004), *The Times* Books, the *Evening Standard* and occasional articles in other newspapers. She has written on a wide variety of topics that tend to be subjects about which she has a lot of knowledge – such as the book world – or things she feels passionate about – such as the erosion of the countryside. Drawing on both her biblical knowledge and her love of storytelling, for example, her *Times* column of Saturday 9 December 2006 provided a modern interpretation of the Christmas story. Winterson frequently returns to the subject of the importance and power of books. In her *Times* column of 16 June 2007, she compares books to the radio telescope at Jodrell Bank, calling them 'transmitters of energy'. Written on the occasion of the first Jodrell Bank Literary Festival, she writes, 'Thank God for books – far from being outdated, they are one of the last places allowing people to sit down and think for themselves (p. 3).' In the same column the following month she analyses the Harry Potter phenomenon, praising the series for getting children to read and participate in a wider culture, but registering misgivings about its imaginative limitations – 'Harry World is very crowded', she concludes (21 July 2007). An earlier column on the 'future of the book' predicted that books 'will go back to being art objects' as other forms of technology deliver text and more and more information is digitalized (*Times*, 4 February 2006, p. 3). Despite, or rather because of, her respect for the book, Winterson believes that far too many books are being published to the detriment of what she calls 'real books'. Singling out 'celebrity biographies' for particular criticism, she recommends that such 'books that don't need to be books' be made available as digital downloads. As with the arguments she puts forward in *Art Objects*, Winterson draws a firm and somewhat elitist distinction between high and popular culture, although she does not say whether she believes popular *fiction* should adopt a digital format. She sounds a note of caution with this argument, however: the pace of technology makes it harder for people to keep track and maintain the integrity of information, whereas books possess a valuable permanency and accessibility which makes them harder to 'lose'. As she concludes, 'There's nothing more democratic than a book' (*Times*, 2006, p. 3). Whatever their format, Winterson avers, books 'will last forever, for the simple reason that we want them in our lives' (*Times*, 10 September 2005, p. 3).

In an interesting column from 4 March 2006 on authorship, originality and rewriting, Winterson tackles the controversy surrounding *The Da Vinci Code* plagiarism court case. The article poses the question 'Is Dan Brown riffing and recreating, or is he pot-boiling with someone else's onions?' (2006, p. 3). Although she famously went to court to win back her domain name (see below), Winterson defends Dan Brown's use of the storyline, if not the book's literary merits, asking 'who owns the copyright to a story-line?' Showing herself to be an astute literary historian, Winterson observes, 'It was the Romantics who have taught us to value originality in the modern sense', and she echoes T.S Eliot's view when she states, 'New work is directly made out of what exists already, but it must bear the unmistakeable mark of its reincarnation' (*ibid.*). For Winterson, the latter is clearly to be more readily found in poetry than the 'mass-market insanity' represented by sales of Brown's book (*ibid.*).

As readers of her fiction are aware, Winterson likes to write about cities, treating them as living entities. In her *Times* column of 18 August 2007, she writes about London, particularly her part of it, Spitalfields in the East End. She evokes the rich history of the area, from the Huguenots fleeing persecution in France in the seventeenth century to its current incarnation as Bangla Town, calling it 'a treasure trove of time' (p. 3). Characteristically, books become her guide to the city; she reviews Rachel Lichtenstein's *On Brick Lane*, 'a quirky and selective history of the street and its environs, concentrating on its Jewish history and Muslim makeover' (p. 3). Despite increasing bourgeoisification, Winterson contends that the place maintains a strange and troubled quality in which the echoes of the past are still alive:

> Some places are protean, and seem unable to fix in time. Spitalfields is such a place, the winds of the Elizabethan cart tracks visible under the

Georgian symmetry, the ruins of the priory hospital – the spital in the
fields, under the old market and built on top of Roman remains.

(p. 3)

Another of Winterson's favourite cities is Venice and in an article from 5 May 2007 Winterson looks back to the writing of
her Venice novel, *The Passion*, which she admits to writing before
actually visiting the city (*Times*, 5 May 2007). Eschewing realism,
Winterson based her account of the city on her reading of Ruskin's
The Stones of Venice of 1851; Jan Morris's 1960 guide, *Venice*; and
Italo Calvino's *Invisible Cities* (1972), a key influence on her work.
Twenty years later, having made repeated trips, she declares herself
still in love with Venice, and celebrates its literary history and carnival character: 'Venice is quantum, a Schrödinger's cat of a city,
simultaneously dead and alive, true and false, solid and watery,
firm and disappeared' (*Times*, 5 May, 2007, p. 8). As she observes,
'Venice offers endless imaginative possibilities' (*ibid.*). After writing *The Passion*, Winterson visited the city to see if what she had
written was true: 'Yes, it was true, and inevitable that there should
be a gondolier's daughter born with webbed feet', she writes
mischievously, adding 'I'm telling you stories. Trust me.' (*ibid.*).

JEANETTEWINTERSON.COM

Winterson was one of the first writers to set up a personal website following a famous court battle in 2000 over ownership of
her domain name which had been bought by a Cambridge academic along with 130 other names (see Harvey, 2000). Winterson
won the case: 'I couldn't have cared less about the web' until
then, she states, but 'it turned out to be the landmark case for
domain name theft' (*Times*, 10 September 2005, p. 3). JeanetteWin-
terson.com has been running since September 2000 and is one of
the best writers' sites available, receiving a reported 20,000 hits
per month.[4] Winterson clearly understands the need to have a
strong online presence because of the opportunities it affords for
promoting her work and communicating with the widest number
of readers. She also understands that as a largely visual medium
the website has to look good and she regularly 'revamps' it; in
her own words, 'throwing money at it to make it sexy' ('*Saturday
Live*' 2007). It now includes a monthly column, excerpts from her
books, links to interviews, a message board and uses audio, images

and Flash movies to present the material in a dynamic and appealing way. Winterson is rightly proud of the site and pokes gentle fun at other writers who have not developed their sites: 'It helps if the site doesn't look like a scroll-down information sheet for a VD clinic' (*Times*, 10 September 2005). Talking to Libby Brooks in 2000, Winterson's enthusiasm was evident: 'It feels exciting, risky, it feels new. I love the web. I love email, I like the swiftness of it' (Brooks, 2000). In a more recent interview published in *The Essential Guide*, Winterson tempers this enthusiasm in a more measured assessment of the web and its impact on her work:

> I don't think technology can change your attitude. I think it's simply something that you use or not depending on where you live in the world and how you live in the world. The Web doesn't matter to me. What matters to me is that people should go on having creative ideas and go on producing interesting work. How they do it, and how they disseminate it is really unimportant. I don't care if books end up being electronic . . . what matters is what's in them, and not necessarily the form that they take.
>
> (Reynolds and Noakes, 2003, p. 28)

More recently, in 2007, she has argued that the two media are complementary and similarly concerned with communication and connection. 'Books and the web are perfectly matched', she writes, and 'Websites are valuable ways of enjoying what we don't know' (*Times*, 10 September 2005, p. 3).

Reflecting on Winterson's relationship to postmodernism, Morrison views Winterson's website as an important facet of her postmodern persona, arguing that it represents 'an authentically hypertextual construct within which [her works'] play with sex, disguise and virtuality is pursued in different ways' (2006, p. 171). Whereas Winterson has repeatedly privileged the book even while lauding the Internet for its communicative possibilities, Morrison points out that 'The site interestingly extends the questions of authorship and authority [the texts] raise, manifesting, through its very form, the dialogism to which Winterson's more traditional authored material can only allude' (2006, p. 171). Observing how Winterson's website facilitates the play of disguises also performed in her texts, he concludes, 'If the figure of the writer herself provides the focus for the site, jeanettewinterson.com itself is woven of a multiplicity of threads, ranging from the literary to the educational to the spiritual to the libidinal' (2006, p. 172).[5]

NEW WORK

In her website column for September 2007, Winterson promotes her novel *The Stone Gods*, which utilizes the science fiction genre. She describes it as 'a book about a broken world and the discovery of a new planet', which represents 'a response to where we are now, and where this now might be taking us' (Winterson, September, 2007, online). Inspired by the radio telescope at Jodrell Bank, which was installed in 1957, the novel is set partly in the future and describes how the now abandoned radio telescope picks up a mysterious signal that is repeated again and again. In one episode the narrator, Billie Crusoe, climbs onto the dis-used dish:

> I felt as though I was in the cup of some giant creature, long extinct. Or a creature that had moved glacier-slow over the land and at last come to a stop here, and slowly fallen asleep, in a deep trance of millennia, waiting to wake again, for the Sun, for some other star, to stir it from unknown dreams.
>
> (*SG*, 2007, p. 185)

In a recent Radio 4 interview she elaborated on this theme, saying that the novel concerned the 'destruction of the natural world and people's desire to start again' (*Saturday Live*). Like *Tanglewreck*, then, the novel is informed by Winterson's concerns about our relationship with the environment. It develops her major themes of 'displacement, searching and longing' in a new social context. In treating contemporary social issues so directly, this work would appear to represent a real departure for Winterson, who acknowledges that

> This is the first time in my working life as a writer that I have felt compelled to work directly with the material in front of me – by that I mean the state of the world [. . .] Well, this is not a time to be a bystander. It is time to make a response. That is what I will do now for the rest of my life.
>
> (Winterson, 2007, online)

This looks to be a new development in a career that has ranged widely in terms of genre and medium while showing a remarkable consistency of theme and subject matter. In a linked move, she has also started up a MySpace blog[6] to provide a platform to debate global and environmental issues. Other forthcoming projects include the BBC adaptation of *Tanglewreck*; and a libretto based on her recent novella *Weight* which she hopes to turn into an opera (Kellaway, 2006). With Margaret Reynolds, Winterson has recently edited new editions of Woolf's nine novels for Vintage. For each volume she commissioned two short essays, one by a writer and one by critic or scholar. In addition, a second novel for children is due out with Bloomsbury in 2008. Carrying on the science fiction theme of *The Stone Gods*, the book is called *Robot Love* and concerns a girl who builds a multi-gendered robot, which kills her parents, after which the pair go on the run. 'I'm fascinated by artificial intelligence and where it will lead', states Winterson (Else and Harris, 2007). Twenty two years after the publication of *Oranges*, Jeanette Winterson is busier than ever.

8

CRITICAL RECEPTION

The subject of intense media scrutiny at times, as Gavin Keulks points out, Winterson has been 'notoriously maligned' by her critics (2007, p. 146). From the start, Winterson has been identified with a wide range of personae including the 'bright young thing' of the mid-1980s, the arrogant lesbian *enfant terrible* of the mid-1990s, and the benign fairy godmother of recent times. Among press coverage there has without doubt been an unwarranted and inordinate focus on her personality and sexuality, characterized by a lurid fascination with her sex life and her supposed female coterie. Examples of hostile reviewing in the mainstream press, particularly but not exclusively by male critics, are legion (Lambert, 1998, online). Mainstream media commentary has consistently elided the distinction between her life and art and, as Lambert notes, the prurient focus on her sexuality and 'arrogant' behaviour has been at the expense of what Winterson calls 'the work' (*ibid.*).

From an academic perspective, Cath Stowers argues that media coverage has created a 'pathologizing of her life story in which her work often almost disappears' (1995, p. 139). Perhaps this confusion between life and art is inevitable given the way in which her fiction draws on aspects of her own autobiographical experience, and given the strong, first-person, unmistakeably Wintersonian voice regardless of setting, theme or character. As Lynne Pearce (1998) and Jago Morrison (2006) acknowledge, Winterson's work has also evoked a certain critical anxiety in some readings. Critics sometimes apologize for aspects of her work (see Pearce, 1998), or criticize perceived shortcomings of her work (see Grice and Woods, 1998). Susana Onega (2006) argues that at least one scholar's approach is characterized by defensiveness. This chapter examines how academic critics have negotiated the difficulty of separating Winterson the individual from Winterson the novelist, traversing what Morrison has called the 'divergence between Winterson's own claims for her writing and the different uses to which it has been put by her various reading publics' (2006, p. 170). As he points out, it is clear that Winterson resists the roles assigned to her, including those of a postmodernist and lesbian writer (p. 170).

As considered earlier, although not immediately a best-seller, *Oranges* gained the rare distinction of being acclaimed by both the popular press and the broadsheet reviewers (Hinds, 1992). By the time of the television adaptation of the novel, at the end of the decade, Winterson was treated as a serious author by the literary establishment *and* enjoyed a large popular following as her sales, readings and fan mail testified. Eminent fellow writers were full of praise: Gore Vidal called her 'the most interesting young writer I have read in 20 years' and Muriel Spark hailed her as a 'fresh voice with a mind behind it' (Jaggi, 2004, online). Winterson won various awards for her early work including the Whitbread Prize for Best First Novel for *Oranges*; the John Llewellyn Rhys Memorial Prize for *The Passion*; and the E.M. Forster Award from the American Academy of Arts and Letters for *Sexing the Cherry*. She was subsequently named among Granta's Best Young Novelists of 1993 and won a reputation as 'one of the most talented of her generation' (*ibid.*). Moreover, her high profile as a lesbian made her critical and popular success particularly significant for lesbian and feminist readers and critics. As Hinds attests,

> That an author who is a lesbian and a feminist should be so successful in such contrasting contexts is seen by other lesbians and feminists as something to celebrate. Whatever misgivings may be felt about the traps and pitfalls of the mainstream, the sight of 'one of us' being given so much approval by the pillars of the establishment, whence usually comes opprobrium, is a source of enormous pleasure.
>
> (1992, p. 153)

Hinds's reservations were prophetic. Earlier, in 1991, Rebecca O'Rourke had cautioned about the fate of an openly lesbian writer in the mainstream: 'By being such a public figure, Jeanette Winterson came in for a lot of privately expressed criticism'

(1991, p. 63). O'Rourke also criticized Winterson for being 'hurried into print' so soon after *Oranges*, with the 'silly' *Boating for Beginners* and the 'fatuous' keep-fit book *Fit for the Future*, and applauded her decision to change publishers as she 'struggled out of the ghastly mess she'd got herself into' (p. 64).

The publication of *Written on the Body* in 1992 was met with much negative criticism, with very few seeing it as the substantial and innovative work that it in hindsight represents. This spelled the beginning of Winterson's 'dark years', in which academic as well as mainstream critics appeared to abandon her (see Pearce, 1998). As Angela Lambert avers, Winterson's work was 'castigated for being boring or incomprehensible' (1998) and she was generally seen as losing her way (Gerrard, 1994). Winterson's self-promotion came in for increasing criticism, especially after she nominated herself as Best Contemporary Writer and named her own novel as Book of the Year in 1992, and she was repeatedly accused of arrogance and egocentrism. The intense media backlash against Winterson lasted for much of the 1990s, and 'her next two fiction works [were] greeted with blanket hostility and ridicule' (Brooks, 2000, online). As Libby Brooks put it, 'Jeanette Winterson took off like a meteor with her magical first novel but then fell to earth under the weight of vitriolic personal attack' (*ibid.*).

Mainstream critics no doubt saw her as a troublesome feminist and some feminists saw her as arrogant and 'unsisterly' in pushing herself forward and blowing her own trumpet. No doubt about it, her work has largely invoked a 'love it or hate it' response. Interestingly, a group of feminist women novelists came to Winterson's defence. Rachel Cusk's review of *Art & Lies* (1994), Marianne Wiggins' review of *Gut Symmetries* (1997) and Michèle Roberts' review of *The PowerBook* (2000) all made positive comments about her work of this period. Cusk, for example, described Winterson's writing as, by turns, 'dazzling', 'moving' and 'genuinely new', adding that 'Winterson's belief in love, beauty and most of all language is evangelical and redemptive' (Cusk, 1994, online). While not wholeheartedly approving her achievement, they clearly sympathized with her attempts to remake language and break away from (gender) stereotypes.

Notwithstanding the hostile press coverage throughout the 1990s, and the fact that her reputation as an outspoken public figure and lesbian came increasingly to dominate reception of her work, Winterson actually diversified her writing and broadcasting output considerably, writing film scripts, journalism, and starting a highly successful website (and famously fighting in the courts for her domain name), which increased her popular fan base enormously. In the print media, Winterson's reputation finally began to improve in the new millennium after the publication of *The PowerBook* in 2000. Although criticized by Elaine Showalter (2000) for being out of touch with the big subjects of the day, it was generally perceived as marking a turning point in her career (Brooks, 2000). Kate Kellaway, for example, said Winterson was too 'witty, original and good a writer' to let her readers down, and called her writing in *PowerBook* 'graceful, jargon-free and light as thistledown' (Kellaway, 2000, online). Reviews of subsequent works – *Lighthousekeeping* (2004), *Weight* (2005) and the children's novel *Tanglewreck* (2006) – have been mixed but generally positive. *Lighthousekeeping* (2004) was called a 'flawed return to form' and 'a slim but lovely Winterson classic' by Joanna Briscoe in *The Guardian* (Briscoe, 2004). *Weight* (2005) garnered mixed reviews, from lukewarm to highly favourable; Stevie Davies praised its 'exquisitely filmic prose that is almost mythopoetic' (Davies, 2006). Geraldine Bedell admired *Tanglewreck*, calling it 'an exceptional book: big, ambitious and awash with Winterson's usual inventiveness' and commenting that writing for children 'seems to have lent warmth to Winterson's voice' (Bedell, 2006). By the end of 2007, and the publication of her latest novel, *The Stone Gods*, Winterson appears to have re-established her reputation as a serious writer with the print media. Although expressing reservations about what she sees as Winterson's dismissive attitude to science fiction and an overly sentimental love story, Ursula Le Guin welcomed the novel as a complex, vivid and cautionary tale – 'or, more precisely a keen lament for our irremediably incautious species' (Le Guin, 2007). Matt Thorne, writing in *The Independent on Sunday*, concluded that

> Ultimately, *The Stone Gods* neither satisfies as science fiction nor as a literary novel that does anything new with genre. Nevertheless, it is the first Winterson novel to surprise in many years, and may yet win her deserved attention from new readers outside her committed circle of fans.

(Thorne, 2007, online)

Winterson has cannily set up a linked MySpace campaign ensuring that her popular fan base remains as buoyant as ever.

Academic critics seem not to have maintained their early enthusiasm for Winterson's work. In *The Cambridge Guide to Literature in English*, Dominic Head identifies Winterson's fiction as notable for 'formal experimentation', 'polemical feminist politics' and 'attention to the boundaries between psychological states of being' (2006, p. 1212). This summarizes the two main paradigms for understanding her work in the academy, postmodernism and (lesbian) feminism. The major debates among Winterson scholars are concerned with two related questions: how far can she be described as a lesbian-feminist writer, and how far can she be described as a postmodernist? As Morrison observes,

> Winterson began to be recognised in the early to mid-1990s by lesbian feminist critics such as Laura Doan, Gabriele Griffin and Cath Stowers as a writer who provided new opportunities to pursue debates around gender, sexuality and literary representation. By the end of the decade she was widely regarded as one of our pre-eminent producers of sophisticated, provocative, unruly postmodern-feminist fiction.
>
> (2006, p. 169)

While both terms were more or less confidently ascribed to her work up to the late 1990s, increasingly they have been called into question as appropriately describing her recent work, not simply because of Winterson's own ambivalence towards them. Among the postmodern critics are those who view her deconstruction of binary oppositions as not going far enough (Doan, 1994, Grice and Woods, 1998), while feminist critics have sometimes viewed her work as suffering from an excess of textualism at the expense of the material (Armitt, 2007). As Paulina Palmer has noted, Winterson's work evinces 'a tension between the lesbian/feminist and the postmodern' (2001, p. 182). Among feminist critics, opinion is quite strongly divided between second wave and third wave feminist approaches. Gabriele Griffin's (1994) early essay established Winterson as a vibrant lesbian-feminist voice, raising expectations that her work would continue in that vein. While third wave feminists tend to celebrate Winterson's 'queer turn' and her performative conception of gender (Doan, 1994; Lindenmeyer, 1999), second wave critics evince more ambivalence about her decentring of the woman's voice and perspective (Pearce, 1998; Armitt, 2007). Interestingly, however, Winterson's work has been seen as simultaneously inimical to and expressive of a radical feminist perspective: Rachel Wingfield (1998) claims that Winterson's work exploits and undermines second wave feminism by espousing a damaging liberal individualism, whereas Stowers (1995, 1996), utilizing post-structuralist and French feminist theories, sees her work as celebrating communities of women and promoting a form of écriture féminine.

The lesbian-feminist reading of Winterson was established in Griffin's 1994 reading of *Oranges* which emphasized the novel's 'defiant lesbian hero' and its 'counter-narrative of men as insignificant and/or grotesque' (Griffin, 1994, p. 83). Griffin's lesbian aesthetic privileges identity politics and positive images, but while these aspects continued to be highlighted in readings of Winterson's work throughout the 1990s, they also give way to a more fragmented concept of identity as difference (see Armitt, 2007). For example, in another early essay, Laura Doan traced the development of a 'lesbian postmodern' aesthetic in Winterson's work of the 1980s, highlighting its deconstruction of gender binaries and the queering of master narratives of Church and family. Yet, Doan also emphasizes the celebration of lesbian existence, something that she sees persisting in Winterson's work of the 1980s:

> [T]he women of Jeanette Winterson's imagination still discover ecstasy with one another rather than with the male companion a conventional telos demands. None of the twelve dancing princesses in *Sexing the Cherry* (1989) finds ultimate happiness with a prince. When the prince isn't homosexual himself and when princely husbands aren't murdered in a surprising and grotesque manner, the princesses explore, in richly poetic imagery, a startling array of unconventional liaisons, from "salty bliss" with a mermaid to a happy lesbian arrangement in Rapunzel's tower . . . As with *Oranges*, where the reconceptualization of the normal makes lesbian existence possible by, in effect, reversing the dominant culture's definition of natural and unnatural . . . Winterson stalls any potential charge of transgression . . . by appropriating the very terms that legitimize heterosexual union.
>
> (Doan, 1994, p. 138)

Readings inspired by French feminism, demonstrated in the criticism of Stowers among others, are compelling. Stowers identifies symbolic female worlds, a critique of phallocentrism and examples of writing the body with associated metaphors of fluidity and the permeability of boundaries. In particular, she traces examples of Luce Irigaray's notion of *le parler femme* – emerging when women speak together without the presence of men – in *Sexing the Cherry*. She notes that Winterson's texts contain journeys which frequently 'lead to female realms, communities of women' (1996, p. 72), and asks, 'what purpose do metaphors of travel, alternative geographies, castaway groups of women, serve in Winterson's work?' Stowers links them to a French feminist 'concern to reclaim femininity and woman, to write both onto the patriarchal map' (1996, p.72). Discussing the representation of female community in *The Passion* and *Sexing*, Stowers writes,

> Such communities effect an excavation of the feminine; are associated with new configurations of space, time, self and gender; are a major motif of lesbian aesthetics; and enable experimental excursions into a female imaginary connected to notions of a pre-Oedipal, maternal realm and a new female language. Whether suggesting a more subtle, unanticipated power or tending towards more blatant separatist concepts, self-contained collectivities of women become emblems of female self-sufficiency and freedom.
>
> (1996, p. 69)

Stowers has been at the forefront of critical efforts to resist the depoliticization of Winterson's work, objecting that 'Winterson's lesbianism is also frequently de-centred or disavowed in the reception of her texts' and arguing forcefully that 'these novels involve a discourse of lesbian desire and are not separable from sexual politics or lesbian specificities, historical and political' (1996, p. 70). Indeed, in Winterson's short story 'The Poetry of Sex', which describes an island nation of women separate from the mainland of men, Stowers finds an illustration of the political motif of Lesbian Nation:

> Remote, floating in that water associated with the feminine and the maternal, this is a realm enabling the emergence of women's multiplicity and diversity. [. . .] The implications of such island imagery are clear; alluding to that original Sapphic isle of the female erotic imagination, and highlighting the marginality of lesbianism in patriarchal society.
>
> (1996, p. 74)

Another critic who has highlighted the presence of lesbian literary tradition in Winterson's work is Heather Nunn. In an article
on *Written*, invoking Kristeva's concept of abjection, Nunn traces
the intertextual references to Wittig's *The Lesbian Body*, arguing that
'the narrator's love-making performs an inversion that reveals the
so-called integrated body as fully disintegrated. There are no stable surfaces on these lesbian bodies as the inner and outer fuse
and mingle' (1996, p. 25). It seems clear that despite Winterson's
protestations to the contrary and sceptical views of certain feminist critics (see Pearce, 1998; Armitt, 2007), Winterson's work
continues to resonate with lesbian-feminist readers.

While simultaneously paying close attention to her literary technique, Palmer has consistently foregrounded both the
feminist-political and the postmodern-theoretical aspects of
Winterson's work in a range of books and articles. In a 2001 essay,
Palmer argues that Winterson utilizes postmodern strategies not
in a random way but for clearly feminist and sexual-political
ends in order to challenge patriarchal values and institutions
(2001, p. 182). Highlighting Winterson's use of strategies of deconstruction, denaturalization and intertextual rewriting of narrative
forms across *Oranges*, *The Passion* and *Sexing*, Palmer argues that

> Winterson's fiction [...] is composed of contraries – ones which
> are particularly difficult to reconcile. Agent/subject, lesbian-feminist/
> postmodern, are two of the antitheses which inform her novels. The
> precise relationship between these contrary sets of terms, whether it
> reflects tension or reconciliation, and which term, if either, dominates
> the other, is open to debate.
>
> (2001, p. 189)

Palmer argues that although the emphasis shifts from novel to
novel, Winterson retains a consistent lesbian-feminist stance, a
viewpoint that also informs this study of her work.

In a subsequent essay which contrasts the early *Passion* with
the more recent *PowerBook*, Palmer (2005) considers the development of Winterson's intellectual interests and her viewpoint
on postmodernism. Acknowledging that both texts make use of
postmodern concepts of performativity, storytelling and intertextuality to transform the heterosexist connotations of the romance
genre, Palmer argues that

Whereas in the former [*Passion*] she explores the gay aesthetic related to the closet, in the latter [*PowerBook*] she situates the relationship between two female lovers in virtual reality, a move which enables her to develop her investigation into the performative aspects of gender and subjectivity. And by reworking motifs appropriated not only from other writers' texts but also from her own earlier novel *The Passion*, she develops the device of intertextuality, giving it a playfully self-reflexive slant. By interrelating lesbian and postmodern perspectives, she thus creates an innovative and, in terms of sexual politics, intellectually challenging form of fiction.

(2005, p. 198)

Despite the 13 years separating them, and the fact that one is set in the past and the other in the future, Palmer identifies a remarkable continuity of theme and approach across Winterson's work.

As *Written on the Body* appears to function as a key text in academic assessments of Winterson's work, I will use it as a case study to examine the different approaches to Winterson's oeuvre along the feminist-postmodernist spectrum. For many feminist critics the novel was a disappointment after her debut works. The journalist and writer Natasha Walter pinpointed the difficulty: 'she leaves out the specification of gender, but blurs all the other contours of the narrator's personality. The narrator has no childhood, no colour, no interests, no class and no post – except for a succession of lovers' (Walter, 1992). In other words, (female) readers felt frustrated that they could not identify with the protagonist on the basis of gender. For Patricia Duncker, the frustration extended to sexuality:

> For this reader at least, *Written on the Body* is a text full of lost opportunities. Winterson refuses to write an 'out' lesbian novel . . . Fair enough. But I think loses more than she gains, because the wonderful echo of *The Lesbian Body* stands at the centre of the book . . . a monument to what the text might have been.
>
> (1998, p. 85)

Lucie Armitt argues that in this 'watershed novel' Winterson is no longer the 'champion of feminist resistance' (2007, p. 20). 'The real problem for me here', she writes, 'is that in denying a woman's voice to the active lover/narrator, the only roles left for the unambiguously female character are the more objectifying ones Louise especially epitomizes: beloved on a pedestal, femme fatale' (2007, p. 20). Similarly, as Lynne Pearce ruefully admits, *Written on the Body* was 'the beginning of the end of my special relationship with Jeanette', the moment at which she felt her own lesbian-feminist '(re)-construction of the Winterson narrative persona' could no longer be sustained in the face of Winterson's writing strategies (1996, p. 33). She particularly criticizes what she sees as Winterson's glamorization of cancer and disease.

In contrast to such disenchanted feminist readings, Stowers sees the 'use of a bisexual, ungendered narrator' as a radical attempt to escape from both sex and gender' (1995, p. 150). She highlights the diverse interpretations of 'this contentious figure', and argues that 'although Winterson's narrator is not simply portrayed as a lesbian, s/he still fulfils distinctly lesbian aims', aligning them with what Bonnie Zimmerman has identified as the 'deconstruction' of the lesbian as 'an essentialist . . . being' and 'the reconstruction of her as a subject position' (*ibid.*). Nunn's subtle reading similarly emphasizes the way in which Winterson's narrative strategy deconstructs 'boundaries and identities', working to reclaim the abject, sick, lesbian body. Discussing the controversial narrator figure, she argues that

> [T] narrator fluctuates between both male and female lovers and invokes imagery that suggests the alternation between feminine and masculine positions. This non-gender specific narrator creates an intriguing (yet troubling) space that can be filled in as desires demand. If, as I have done, it is possible to construct the narrator as a woman, then from a theoretical perspective the narrator might be read as a lesbian subject.
>
> (1996, p. 20)

Antje Lindenmeyer (1999) argues that the novel engages with feminist theory and politics on a number of levels. In her 1999 article, Lindenmeyer expertly traced the postmodern concepts of the body in *Written on the Body*: 'On one level', she writes, 'the novel is a straight-forward feminist critique of androcentric science, its image of the female body, and the destructive way in which it strives to penetrate and dissect it. On a further, "postmodern" level, the author disturbs identities, boundaries and gendered identities' (1999, p. 60). In other words, *Written* represents a third wave conception of the (female) body not as 'simply there, untainted by society' or as 'a passive, victimized site of society's inscription', but as a set of multiple parts held together by 'forces of connection' (p. 60).

What seems evident in this complex debate is that there are (at least) two models of lesbian (and female) identity at stake: the first emphasizes identification, affirmation and positive images; the second represents lesbianism as a dissident or transgressive subject position. Both are present in Winterson's work, but arguably the latter comes to predominate as the texts become less and less about discernible lesbian characters.[1] Some critics have begun to challenge both poles of what has become an orthodox lesbian-feminist framework for reading Winterson's work, which sees Winterson as either abandoning her lesbian-feminist aesthetic or pursuing it by other (deconstructive) means. In complete contrast to the lesbian-feminist viewpoint of the theories discussed above, Louise Horskjaer Humphries states, 'I believe she is right when she rejects lesbianism as the key to her fiction' (1999, p. 6). But, perhaps there is a third model at play in Winterson's work, which arguably cuts across the other two. This is the representation of lesbianism, neither as role model nor as dissidence, but as a kind of absent presence, something woven into the narrative, and giving rise to intertextual echoes, but not signifying a particular ideological position.

Picking up on the debate about Winterson's critical reception, Morrison (2006) argues that Winterson has sought, both in her fiction and in her critical writing, to distance her work from the very paradigms set up by academic criticism. Questioning 'the now orthodox reading of Winterson as a queer postmodernist' (p. 171), Morrison identifies an 'ambivalence that runs to the heart of her fiction itself (p. 170). He argues that her recent work has increasingly moved away from the lesbian postmodern aesthetic advanced by Palmer and others to embrace what he sees as a Christian or post-Christian sensibility, which promotes the notion of an ideal, transcendent love:

> In her latest writing especially [. . .] Winterson's indebtedness to this Christian sensibility forces us into a new kind of reading, almost completely foreclosing the lesbian feminist Winterson we have enjoyed and admired. For critics and fans alike [. . .] this leaves us in a strange

position, guarding and conserving an institution of queer postmodernism, whilst at the same time, at a side window, the writer herself seems to be engaged in an escape attempt.

(2006, p. 171)

While Morrison is right to highlight the pervasiveness of Christian symbolism in Winterson's work, and usefully applies Kristeva's distinction between the Christian notion of *agape* love and the Greek concept of *eros*, he arguably overstates the extent to which this model characterizes Winterson's recent oeuvre. Evangelical motifs, tropes of transcendent love and the Christ-figure appear in all her work from *Oranges*, especially *The Passion*, whose very title gestures towards the redemptive power of Christ's love (see Denby, 2007). While Morrison's view that *The PowerBook* undertakes a 'sacrificial shedding of the erotic body itself' is compelling, the novel also celebrates bodily desires and pleasures in a manner totally at odds with Christian asceticism. And while it is true that the lesbian – as either 'defiant hero' (Griffin) or desiring body – plays a smaller part in *Lighthousekeeping* of 2004, nevertheless Morrison mistakes the nature of the novel's sex scene between Silver and her lover. If we read the lover as the *woman* Silver met in Athens, as we are encouraged to do by the use of the second person, the scene – with its 'a flood of heterosexual clichés' (p. 178) – takes on a different meaning, and does indeed break the frame and reverse gender expectations. In all the recent works from *The PowerBook*, Winterson is far from jettisoning earthly pleasures as Morrison claims, and the earthiness of her language is at odds with that of St Augustine. It is the passion of evangelical language that inspires Winterson, not its asceticism.

A contrast to the view that Winterson's work is characterized by the disappearance of the body (Morrison) and/or the disappearance of women (Armitt, 2007) appears in Ina Schabert's 'Habeus Corpus 2000: The Return of the Body', which situates Winterson as one of a number of writers whose work heralds a return of the body in cultural theory and practice, thereby offering a critique of disembodied forms of postmodernism. For Schabert, feminist writers such as Winterson and Michèle Roberts 'press the disembodied mode of writing into the service of presenting, representing, 're-membering' and reliving the body (2001, p. 87). Schabert interprets their use of body writing metaphors as an attempt to experience and represent the body through language. Winterson's work shows how 'signifying practices are embodied practices – the body, the senses, the corporeal memory created by iterative collective and personal bodily experience, all taking part in the production of meaning' (p. 95). *Written on the Body*, according to Schabert, represents a kind of 'mysticism of the body' (p. 105) in which 'sensual and sexual encounters lead up to the intuition of a secret knowledge "that is deeper than consciousness", yet lodged in the body more than held in the mind" (Winterson, 1992, p. 82)' (Schabert, 2001, p. 105 emphasis in original). Schabert compares Winterson's postmodern metaphor of the body as book to medieval illuminated manuscripts, where they are used 'to convey the inseparability of body and soul, of physical existence and intimately personal meaning' (p. 107). Her reading offers a valuable alternative view on the debates about feminist representation and body politics.

In a thought-provoking essay which challenges previous critical assumptions, Louise Horskjaer Humphries states, 'What particularly worries me is that Winterson's writing is weighed against some assumptions about what lesbian writing should and should not do, and subsequently found too light' (1999, p. 7). She concludes that

> Jeanette Winterson is a writer very much taken up with philosophical questions where sex is endlessly significant, but not confined to the directly political. Central to her writing seems to be ontological questions about the creation of identity and the nature of humanity, and, in relation to these, two very significant concerns are those of love and language.
>
> (1999, p. 16)

This perhaps helps to explain Winterson's well-known resistance to the role of spokesperson for women and lesbians; as she told yet another curious interviewer, 'I don't want to be a political writer, or a writer whose concern is sexual politics' (cited in Horskjaer Humphries, 1999, p. 3). One objection is that it is characteristic of writers to reject labels and categories which are, as Butler (2004) reminds us, regulatory regimes, and lesbian-feminist debates will remain among the useful touchstones for Winterson's oeuvre.

Eschewing the ideological terms of the postmodern versus lesbian-feminist debate, some recent critics have opted for a more thematic approach. Peter Childs's chapter on Winterson in his recent book *Contemporary Novelists* identifies Winterson's key themes as 'love, life, the universe and story-telling' and focuses on her self-professed obsession with the nature of 'boundaries and desire' (2005, p. 260). Childs calls Winterson 'an uneven but consistently interesting writer', whose work evinces 'a constancy of theme and focus, despite enormous variety of style and setting, that makes each book appear a variation on familiar preoccupations, teasing away at them in fresh ways using new ideas' (2007, p. 260). He points out the continuities in Winterson's fiction such as the use of the triangular love plot, the idea of love as a precious possession and the representation of history and social reality as social constructs. All these themes are linked to the overriding theme of storytelling which Winterson returns to throughout her fiction: 'To love differently emerges as a goal achieved by telling stories differently, or re-imagining and re-mapping life' (p. 261). Interestingly, here, Childs acknowledges 'difference', but more usually he emphasizes the universal reach of Winterson's themes. Writing just before *Lighthousekeeping* appeared, he advances the view that 'a claim might be made for her recent work expressing a new maturity as she explores love's triangularity using art, science or technology' (p. 260). In contrast to Grice and Woods, he champions *Gut Symmetries* as a richly nuanced narrative that warrants more attention than it has so far received. After giving an overview of her work to date, he focuses on what he sees as the key works: *Oranges* and *Written on the Body*. The chapter is useful (especially for student readers at whom it is aimed) for the work it does in summing up Winterson's thematic concerns across her whole career and placing them in a universalist framework that often gets overlooked in more highly charged and particularist theoretical readings. However, we still need theory to interpret Winterson's treatment of the themes of love, history and storytelling as the rich history of Winterson criticism demonstrates.

Susana Onega's 2006 study takes seriously Winterson's claim to stand in a tradition stretching from the European modernists Eliot, Pound and Woolf to the international experimentalist trend that includes Gabriel García Márquez, Italo Calvino and Isabel Allende. In common with modernists such as Yeats, Eliot and Graves, Onega claims that Winterson's work aims for 'an organic unity' and foregrounds the figure of the 'mythical quester' (2006, p. 7). Onega also highlights the importance of a distinctive female trajectory that begins, once again, with Woolf, and includes Angela Carter, Sara Maitland and Marina Warner. In a claim with which I concur, Onega sees Winterson fulfilling Woolf's 'prophetic dream of a new novelistic form created by women with the intellectual and material freedom to create their own sensibility and worldview' (p. 13); the book adapted to the body. Offering a series of detailed and informative close readings of her texts up to *Lighthousekeeping*, Onega carefully traces Winterson's intertextual allusions to both the Western literary tradition and her own works. Writing just before the publication of *Weight*, and confirming the views of both Palmer and Childs, Onega argues that Winterson evinces a 'continuing interest in the same topoi that recur in her earlier novels' (p. 223). Onega sees Winterson as 'constantly approaching the same subjects and ideas from different perspectives while tying everything to a single central vision' (p. 223). Identifying a new ethics of love and freedom as the key to Winterson's vision, Onega concludes that

> This definition of love, which allows for individual freedom and rejects dogma, accepts alterity in the other as well as in oneself and refuses to draw social and generic distinctions, is the essential element in the novels that provides the stimulus for the characters' life quests and confers meaning on their existence.
>
> (2006, p. 233)

Recently, critics are re-evaluating Winterson's work in the light of more nuanced accounts of contemporary experimental writing and her own apparent attempts in her recent work to reclaim storytelling from postmodern exhaustion. Keulks argues cogently that this 'late-phase (or second-phase) postmodernism . . . forswears the nihilism, ahistoricism and relativism' of the earlier version, and that Winterson's recent fiction provides 'reconstituted versions of history and mythology' which restabilize 'both the emotional present and the historical past' (2007, p. 148). For Keulks, *Lighthousekeeping* represents a significant shift away from the postmodern aesthetic that Winterson pushed to the extreme in *The PowerBook*, but he advises caution in any reassessment of Winterson's work along the realist/postmodern axis:

> Although it is tempting to label *Lighthousekeeping* a realist or at least anti-postmodernist text, the novel remains too tainted by metafiction and intertextuality to be so conveniently positioned. Its realism ultimately genuflects to the grander disorder of textuality.
>
> (2007, p. 153)

For Keulks, therefore, the recent texts, *The PowerBook*, *Lighthousekeeping* and *Weight*, 'can be read as artistic signposts of her shifting relation to realism and postmodernism' (2007, p. 147). Just as academic critics themselves are revising their accounts of postmodernism, then, so Winterson is repositioning her work in relation to contemporary theory and culture. As Keulks concludes,

> Postmodernism is unquestionably part of this 'intolerable' 'burden' [explored in *Weight*], as are autobiography, feminism, celebrity, and all the labels that Jeanette Winterson has attracted. It has formed a large part of the 'orbit' of her past and her present, and it will take great effort to break its 'gravitational pull'. Only subsequent novels will determine the role postmodernism will play in her future.
>
> (2007, p. 160)

Whether we see lesbianism as centred (Stowers) or decentred (Horksjaer Humphries) in Winterson's work, and whether we see her as a predominately modernist or postmodernist writer, it seems clear that Winterson's work has provided the basis for a fascinating and important set of debates around identity, representation and meaning. Arguably, Winterson's work has always called into question identity categories while at the same time tracing the contours of human desire predicated on love for women. As Pearce says, Winterson's work interrogates ideas and assumptions about feminist theories and knowledge, but while Pearce and others have found Winterson wanting, surely one cannot expect her to write to an academic remit, fulfilling our construction of her as 'queer', 'postmodern', 'lesbian' or 'feminist'. Her work resists such containment strategies, and just as we think we get the measure of her, she tries to do something different. She reaches simultaneously for the universal and the particular, finding one in the other, demonstrating that art is artful, and sexy rather than sexed. As Horskjaer Humphries concludes,

> The "Wintersonian poetics" then, seems to be that books are the space in which desire can be explored. [. . .] It is a highly sexy, but not specifically gendered space and irreducible to mapping by way of gender politics or philosophical dualism. It is the space of stories . . . and Winterson's are of the very best.
>
> (1999, p. 16)

NOTES

CHAPTER 1

1. In the UK, Winterson's books have been included in the National Curriculum for Schools since the 1990s and *Oranges* is prescribed reading in the AQA exam board syllabus for A-Level English Literature.
2. For example, Winterson appeared regularly as a guest pundit on *The Culture Show* during the 1990s.
3. This is not the case for British film and television, however, in which social (and comic) realism as a mode flourished in films by Ken Loach, Mike Leigh and Willie Russell, and television programmes like Alan Bleasedale's *Boys from the Blackstuff* and Dick Clement and Ian La Frenais's *Auf Wiedersehen Pet*.
4. See her essay 'The Semiotics of Sex' in *Art Objects*, and her comments in Chapter 6.

CHAPTER 2

1. See *Art Objects* for an account of her purchases in the mid-1990s, pp. 119–132.
2. The Jeanette Winterson Readers' Site run by Anna Troberg can be found at http://web.telia.com

CHAPTER 3

1. Examples include Rita Mae Brown's *Rubyfruit Jungle* (1977), Audre Lorde's *Zami: A New Spelling of My Name* (1982), and Florence King's *Confessions of a Failed Southern Lady* (1985). Although these examples are from the United States, they were all published within a few years of *Oranges* and share many similar features of the lesbian Bildungsroman.
2. Examples of 'escape' narratives include Brown's *Rubyfruit Jungle* and Monique Wittig's *Les Guerillères* (1973).

CHAPTER 4

1. Refers to the representation of women, especially lesbians, as eroticized mirror images of each other. See Reina Lewis (1996).

2. In *S/Z*, Roland Barthes (1990) distinguishes between 'readerly' texts which the reader more or less passively consumes and 'writerly' texts which require the reader to participate in the construction of meaning.
3. The significance of Strauss' *Der Rosenkavalier* (1911) is alluded to earlier in the novel: the female role of Marie Therese, the Marschallin, was coveted by the castrato who was for many years the lover of the Cardinal, who later becomes Handel's lover (p. 196).

CHAPTER 5

1. See *Weight*, p. 131.
2. In fact, Ali's personae function as 'avatars' – identities created by users in virtual reality games such as *Second Life*. Winterson's fictional world anticipated *Second Life*, which began in 2003, by several years.
3. In Greek myth, Tiresius is the blind seer of Thebes. He combines male and female attributes and reveals to Oedipus the truth of his parentage.
4. Stella is one of the two main female characters in *Gut Symmetries*.
5. The postmodern idea that the representation of reality can only be understood as a form of textual play.

CHAPTER 7

1. Winterson has published four Christmas stories for the *Guardian* and a further seven stories are listed on her website, www.jeanettewinterson. com.
2. In 1995 Fiona Shaw performed Deborah Warner's stage version of *The Waste Land* and she has also played *King Lear*.
3. Winterson met her partner Deborah Warner while collaborating on the project.
4. The Official Jeanette Winterson Site can be found at http://www. jeanettewinterson.com/
5. One of the 'libidinal' examples Morrison cites is an online sexual confession by a user who claimed to have slept with the singer K.D Lang (2006, p. 172).
6. See her website for details.

CHAPTER 8

1. Although there are numerous lesbian and lesbian-like characters in the subsequent and later works: Sappho and Picasso in *Art & Lies*, Alice and Stella in *Gut Symmetries*, Ali/Alix in *The PowerBook* and Silver in *Lighthousekeeping*.

BIBLIOGRAPHY

Works by Jeanette Winterson

NOVELS

Oranges Are Not the Only Fruit (London: Pandora, 1985).
Boating for Beginners (London: Methuen, 1985).
The Passion (London: Bloomsbury, 1987).
Sexing the Cherry (London: Bloomsbury, 1989).
Written on the Body (London: Jonathan Cape, 1992).
Art and Lies. A Piece for Three Voices and a Bawd (London: Jonathan Cape, 1994).
G.U.T Symmetries (London: Granta, 1997).
The PowerBook (London: Jonathan Cape 2000).
Lighthousekeeping (London: Fourth Estate, 2004).
Weight (London: Canongate, 2005).
The Stone Gods (London: Hamish Hamilton, 2007)

CHILDREN'S FICTION

The King of Capri (London: Bloomsbury, 2003).
Tanglewreck (London: Bloomsbury, 2006).

SHORT FICTION

The World and Other Places (London: Jonathan Cape, 1998).
'The horse in the snow', *The Guardian*, 24 December 2005.

NON-FICTION WORKS

Fit for the Future: The Guide for Women Who Want to Live Well (London: Pandora, 1986).
Art Objects: Essays on Ecstasy and Effrontery (London: Jonathan Cape, 1995).

SCRIPTS FOR TELEVISION, THEATRE, FILM AND RADIO

Static (radio play). J. Mortimer (ed.), *Young Playwrights Festival* (London: BBC Books, 1998).

Oranges Are Not the Only Fruit: The Script (London: Pandora, 1990).

Shades of Fear (1993). Director: B. Kidron.

Great Moments in Aviation (script) (London:Vintage Film Scripts, 1994).

Text Message. BBC Radio 4. 24 November, 2001. www.bbc.co.uk/radio4/ woman'shour/2001 Accessed on 20 July 2006.

The PowerBook (2003). Director: D. Warner.

INTERVIEWS

Brooks, L. Interview. 'Power surge' *The Guardian*, *G2*, 31 March 2000, p. 3.

Edemariam, A. 'I want to change the world', *The Guardian*, Saturday 29 September 2007. http://books.guardian.co.uk/departments/generalfiction/story/0,,2179826,00.html Accessed on 6 June 2008.

Else, L. and Harris, E. 'In search of a grand unified theory of me', *New Scientist*, 25 August 2007. http://www.jeanettewinterson.com/pages/content/index.asp?PageID=470 Accessed on 6 June 2008.

Jaggi, M. Interview. 'Redemption songs', *The Guardian*, Saturday 29 May 2004. http://books.guardian.co.uk/print/0,3858,4934260-110738,00. html Accessed on 17 April 2004.

Kellaway, K. Interview with 'Jeanette Winterson'. *The Observer*, Sunday 25 June 2006. http://observer.guardian.co.uk/magazine/story/0,,1803744, 00.html Accessed on 2 November 2007.

Lambert, A. 'Interview'. *Prospect Magazine*. February 1998. http://www.prospect-magazine.co.uk/article_details.php?id=4295 Accessed on 11 October 2006.

Miller, L.. 'A mind of one's own'. *The Guardian*, 22 October 2005, p. 11.

Wachel, E. with 'Jeanette Winterson: An interview', *Malahat Review* III (1997), 61–73.

Winterson, J. 'Interview'. *Spare Rib*, 209 1990, 26–29.

'The author of *Oranges Are Not the Only Fruit* and *The PowerBook* discusses gender, identity and why she's a hopeless romantic', *Guardian Unlimited*, Thursday 7 September 2000. <http://www.guardian.co.uk/Archive /Article/> Accessed on 21 July 2003.

Winterson, J. 'Invented Worlds' Programme Notes, stage production of *The PowerBook*. Devised by Jeannette Winterson, Deborah Warner and Fiona Shaw. Lyttleton Theatre, 9 May–4 June 2002.

Winterson, J. 'Interview', Press Conference for *The PowerBook* (Rome: RomaEuropa Festival, 2 October 2003).

Winterson, J. 'From innocence to experience'. Louise Tucker talks to Jeanette Winterson. Appendix to *Lighthousekeeping* (London: Harper-Perennial, 2005), pp. 2–14.

Winterson, J. 'Endless possibilities'. Appendix essay to *Lighthousekeeping* (London: Harperperennial, 2005), pp. 18–23.

Winterson, J. 'Interview'. *Saturday Live* BBC Radio 4, Saturday 6 October 2007.

JOURNALISM

'Clare Balding', *Evening Standard*, September 2005. http://www.jeanette-winterson.com/pages/content/index.asp?PageID=109 Accessed on 2 November 2007.

'Thanks to me, Madonna and Julia Roberts both got their names back'. *Times*, Saturday 10 September 2005, p. 3.

'Let's stop publishing books that don't really need to be books'. *Times*, Saturday 4 February 2006, p. 3.

'The retelling or remaking of any work has to carry the past into the future'. *Times*, Saturday 4 March 2006, p. 3.

'Books are transmitters of the energy of the cosmos'. *Times*, Saturday 16 June 2007, p. 3.

'Only stories can frame this shifting city's stones'. *Times*, Saturday 5 May 2007, p. 8.

'The trouble with Harryworld is that it's a very crowded place'. *Times*, Saturday 21 July 2007, p. 3.

'A place where people disappear and not just at the hands of the Krays'. *Times*, Saturday 18 August 2007, p. 3.

'Kids love enclosed worlds, but they need to be shown what's outside'. *Times*, Saturday 8 December 2007, p. 3.

PERSONAL WEBSITE

'Biography'. http://www.jeanettewinterson.com/pages/cotent/index.asp?PageID=207 Accessed on 28 September 2006.

'September'. http://www.jeanettewinterson.com/pages/content/index.asp?PageID=464 Accessed on 28 September 2007.

WORKS CITED

Ackroyd, P. *Hawksmoor* (London: Abacus, 1986).

Amis, M. *Money: A Suicide Note* (London: Vintage, 2005).

Andermahr, S. (ed.), *Jeanette Winterson: A Contemporary Critical Guide* (London: Continuum, 2007).

Armitt, L. *Contemporary Women's Fiction and the Fantastic* (London: Macmillan, 2000).

Armitt, L. 'Storytelling and Feminism', in S. Andermahr (ed.) *Jeanette Winterson: A Contemporary Critical Guide* (London: Continuum, 2007), pp. 14–26.

Aròstegui, M. Del Mar Ascensio. 'Subversion of sexual identity in Jeanette Winterson's *The Passion*', in C. Cornut-Gentille D'Arcy and J. Àngel Garcìa Landa (eds) *Postmodern Studies 16: Gender, I-Deology, Essays on Theory, Fiction and Film* (Amsterdam: Rodopi, 1996), pp. 265–279.

Atwood, M. *The Penelopiad: The Myth of Penelope and Odysseus* (London: Canongate, 2005).

Bakhtin, M.M. *The Dialogic Imagination: Four Essays*, M. Holquist (ed. and trans.) (Austin: University of Texas, Press, 1981).

Bakhtin, M.M. *Rabelais and His World* (Indiana: Indiana UP, 1984).

Barnes, D. *Nightwood* (London: Faber and Faber, 1987).

Barthes, R. 'The death of the author', in S. Heath (ed.) and trans., *Image-Music-Text* (London: Fontana, 1977).

Barthes, R. *S/Z*, R. Miller. trans. (Oxford: Blackwell, 1990).

Bedell, G. 'Review. "A rabbit called Bigamist? Read on"'. *The Observer*, Sunday 2 July 2006. http:// books.guardian.co.uk/reviews/childrenandteens/0,,1810578,00.html Accessed on 28 September 2006.

Belsey, C. and Moore, J. (eds) *The Feminist Reader* (London: MacMillan, 1989).

Benstock, S. *Women of the Left Bank* (Austin: University of Texas, 1986).

Billington, M. 'Review', *The Guardian*, 20 May 2002.

Blau du Plessis, R. *Writing Beyond the Ending: Narrative Strategies of Twentieth-Century Women Writers* (Bloomington: Indiana UP, 1985).

Blau du Plessis, R. *The Pink Guitar: Writing as Feminist Practice* (London: Routledge, 1990).

Bray, A. *Homosexuality in Renaissance England* (New York: Columbia UP, 1995).

Brockes, E. 'Hollywood snub for Winterson', *The Guardian*, 18 December 2000, p. 6.

Bronfen, E. *Over Her Dead Body: Death, Femininity and the Aesthetic* (Manchester: Manchester UP, 1992).

Bronte, C. *Jane Eyre* (London: Penguin Classics, 2006).

Briscoe, J. 'Full beam ahead'. *The Guardian*, Saturday 8 May 2004. http:// books.guardian.co.uk/reviews/generalfiction/0,6121,1211719,00.html Accessed on 13 July 2005.

Brooker, P. (ed.) *Modernism/Postmodernism* (London: Longman, 1992).

Brown, R.M. *Rubyfruit Jungle* (New York: Bantam Books, 1977).

Butler, J. 'Imitation and gender insubordination', in S. Salih (ed.) *The Judith Butler Reader* (Oxford: Blackwell, 2004), pp. 119–137.

Butler, J. *Bodies that Matter: On the Discursive Limits of Sex* (London: Routledge, 1993).

Calvino, I. *Invisible Cities* (London: Vintage, 1997).

Campbell-Johnstone, R. 'Prophet of the new age'. *The Times*, September 2000, pp. 10–11.

Carpenter, G. 'Reading and the reader', in S. Andermahr (ed.) *Jeanette Winterson: A Contemporary Critical Guide* (London: Continuum, 2007), pp. 69–81.

Carter, A. *Nights at the Circus* (London: Vintage, 1994).

Castle, T. 'Sylvia Townsend Warner and the counter-plot of Lesbian Fiction', *Textual Practice* 2(4) (Summer 1990), pp.213–235.

Childs, P. 'Jeanette Winterson: boundaries and desire', in *Contemporary Novelists: British Fiction Since 1970* (London: Palgrave Macmillan, 2005), pp. 255–273.

Cixous, H. 'Sorties', in E. Marks and I. De Courtivron (eds) *New French Feminisms: An Anthology* (Hemel Hempstead: Harvester Wheatsheaf, 1981), pp. 90–98.

Cixous, H. 'The Laugh of the medusa', in E. Marks and I. De Courtivron (eds) *New French Feminisms: An Anthology* (Hemel Hempstead: Harvester Wheatsheaf, 1981), pp. 245–264.

Cleland, J. *Memoirs of a Woman of Pleasure* (Oxford: Oxford University Press, 1999).

Cooper, D. *Meridian*. BBC Radio 4. 18 June, 1986.

Cusk, R. 'A wretchedness new to history'. *The Times*, 20 June 1994.

Davies, S. 'Of Gods and mythical monsters' *The Independent*, 28 October 2005. http://enjoyment.independent.co.uk/books/reviewsarticles 322672.ece Accessed on 28 September 2006.

Darwin, C. *On the Origin of Species* (London: Wordsworth, 1998).

De Jongh, N. 'Review'. *Evening Standard*, 20 May 2002.

De Lauretis, T. 'Queer theory: lesbian and gay sexualities: An introduction'. *Differences: A Journal of Feminist Cultural Studies*, 3(2) (1991), iii–xviii.

Denby, M. 'Religion and spirituality', in S. Andermahr (ed.) *Jeanette Winterson: A Contemporary Critical Guide* (London: Continuum, 2007), pp. 100–113.

Doan, L. 'Sexing the postmodern', in L. Doan (ed.) *The Lesbian Postmodern* (New York: Columbia UP, 1994), pp. 137–155.

Duncker, P. 'Jeanette Winterson and the aftermath of feminism', in H. Grice and T. Woods (eds) *'I'm Telling You Stories': Jeanette Winterson and the Politics of Reading* (Amsterdam: Rodopi, 1998), pp. 77–88.

Dunn, J. *The John Dunn Show*. BBC Radio 2, 4 January 1990.

Eliot, T.S. 'Tradition and the individual talent', in *Selected Essays 1917–32* (London: Harcourt, Brace and Company, 1932).

Emck, K. 'Gut Symmetries'. *Times Literary Supplement*, 3 January 1997, p. 21.

Forster, E.M. *Howard's End* (London: Penguin, 1968).

Foucault, M. 'What is an author?' in J.V. Harari (ed.) *Textual Strategies: Perspectives in Post-Structuralist Criticism* (London: Methuen, 1980).

Fowles, J. *The French Lieutenant's Woman* (London: Granada, 1977).

Freely, M. 'God's gift to women'. *The Observer*, 20 August, 2000, p. 27.

Freud, S. 'Mourning and melancholia,' in J. Strachey (ed.) and trans. Standard Edition of the Complete Psychological *Works of Sigmund Freud*, Vol. 14. (London: Hogarth, 1957), pp. 243–258.

Gerrard, N. 'The ultimate self-produced woman,' *The Observer*, 5 June 1994.

Grice, H. and Woods, T. 'Grand (dis)unified theories? Dislocated Discourses in *Gut Symmetries*', in H. Grice and T. Woods (eds) *'I'm Telling You Stories': Jeanette Winterson and the Politics of Reading* (Amsterdam: Rodopi, 1998), pp. 117–126.

Grice, H. and Woods, T. 'Winterson's dislocated discourses,' in S. Andermahr (ed.) *Jeanette Winterson: A Contemporary Critical Guide* (London: Continuum, 2007), pp. 27–40.

Griffin, G. 'Acts of defiance: Celebrating Lesbians', in G. Wisker (ed.) *It's My Party: Reading Twentieth Century Women's Writing* (London: Pluto, 1994).

Gustar, J. 'Language and the limits of desire,' in S. Andermahr (ed.) *Jeanette Winterson: A Contemporary Critical Guide* (London: Continuum, 2007), pp. 55–68.

Hall, R. *The Well of Loneliness* (London: Virago, 1982).

Haraway, D. 'A manifesto for cyborgs', in L.J. Nicholson (ed.) *Feminism/Postmodernism* (New York and London: Routledge, 1990).

Harthill, R. 'Writers revealed', Radio 4, Autumn, 1990.

Harvey, M. 'Novelist wins back her name'. *The Times*, 25 May 2000, p. 11.

Head, D. (ed.) *The Cambridge Guide to Literature in English* (Cambridge: Cambridge University Press, 2006).

Hinds, H. 'Oranges are not the only fruit: Reaching audiences other texts cannot reach', in S. Munt (ed.) *New Lesbian Criticism: Literary and Cultural Readings* (Hemel Hempstead: Harvester Wheatsheaf, 1992), pp.153–172.

Horskjaer Humphries, L. 'Listening for the author's voice: 'Unsexing' the Wintersonian oeuvre', in H. Bengtson, M. Borch, and C. Maagard (eds) *Sponsored by Demons: The Art of Jeanette Winterson* (Odense, Denmark: Scholar's Press, 1999), pp. 3–16.

Humm, M. *Feminisms: A Reader* (Hemel Hempstead: Harvester Wheat-sheaf, 1992).

Hutcheon, L. *A Poetics of Postmodernism* (New York & London: Routledge, 1988).

Hutcheon, L. *The Politics of Postmodernism* (New York & London: Routledge, 1989).

Irigaray, L. *This Sex Which Is Not One*, C. Porter with C. Burke trans. (Ithaca, NY: Cornell University Press, 1985).

Irigaray, L. 'When our lips speak together', in J. Price and M. Shildrick (eds) *Feminist Theory and the Body: A Reader* (Edinburgh: Edinburgh UP, 1999), pp. 82–90.

Ishiguro, K. *Remains of the Day* (London: Faber and Faber, 1989).

Jackson, R. *Fantasy: A Literature of Subversion* (London: Routledge, 1981).

Kellaway, K. 'She's got the power', *The Observer*, Sunday 27 August 2000. http://books.guardian.co.uk/reviews/generalfiction/0,6121,359570,00.html Accessed on 21 July 2003.

Keulks, G. 'Winterson's recent work: Navigating realism and postmod-ernism', In S. Andermahr (ed.) *Jeanette Winterson: A Contemporary Critical Reader* (London: Palgrave Macmillan, 2007), pp. 146–162.

King, F. *Confessions of a Failed Southern Lady* (London: Black Swan, 1985).

Klein, Y.M. 'Myth and community in recent Lesbian autobiographical fiction', K. Jay, J. Glasgow, and C.R. Stimpson (eds) *Lesbian Texts and Contexts: Radical Revisions* (New York: New York University Press, 1990).

Kosofsky Sedgwick, E. *Tendencies* (Hemel Hempstead: Harvester Wheat-sheaf, 1994).

Kristeva, J. 'The system and the speaking subject', in T. Moi (ed.) *The Kristeva Reader* (Oxford: Basil Blackwell, 1986), pp. 24–33.

Kristeva, J. *Powers of Horror: An Essay on Abjection*, L.S. Roudiez trans. (New York: Columbia University Press, 1982).

Lacan, J. *Ecrits: A Selection*, A. Sheridan trans (London: Routledge/Tavistock, 1977).

Le Guin, U. 'Head cases' *The Guardian*, Saturday 22 September 2007. http://books.guardian.co.uk/reviews/sciencefiction/0,,2174334,00.html Acc-essed on 6 January 2008.

Lessing, D. *The Golden Notebook* (London: Panther, 1973).

Lewis, R. and Rolley, K. 'Ad(dressing) the Dyke: Lesbian looks and Lesbians looking', in P. Horne and R. Lewis (eds) *Outlooks: Les-bian and Gay Sexualities and Visual Cultures* (London: Routledge, 1996), pp. 178–190.

Lichtenstein, R. *On Brick Lane* (London: Hamish Hamilton, 2007).

Lindenmeyer, A. 'Postmodern concepts of the body in Jeanette Winterson's *Written on the Body*', *Feminist Review* 63 (Autumn 1999), 48–63.

Lorde, A. *Zami: A New Spelling of My Name* (Trumansberg, NY: Crossing Press, 1982).

Lyotard, J.-F. *The Postmodern Condition: A Report on Knowledge* (Manchester: Manchester UP, 1984).

Makinen, M. *The Novels of Jeanette Winterson: A Reader's Guide to Essential Criticism* (Basingstoke: Palgrave, 2005).

Marshall, B.K. *Teaching the Postmodern: Fiction and Theory* (London: Routledge, 1992).

Marshment, M. and Hallam, J. ' "From strings of knots to orangebox": Lesbianism on primetime', in D. Hamer and B. Budge (eds) *The Good, the Bad and the Gorgeous: Popular Culture's Romance with Lesbianism* (London: Pandora, 1994), pp. 142–165.

Millett, K. *Sexual Politics* (London: Virago, 1970).

Montgomery, M., Durant, A., Fabb, N., Furniss, T., and Sara, M. (eds) *Ways of Reading: Advanced Reading Skills for Students of English Literature* (London: Routledge, 1992).

Morris, J. *Venice* (London: Faber and Faber, 2004).

Morrison, J. 'Who cares about gender at a time like this? Love, sex and the problem of Jeanette Winterson', *Journal of Gender Studies* 15(2) (2006), 169–180.

Mueller, M. 'Love and other dismemberments in Jeanette Winterson's novels', in B. Neumeier (ed.) *Endgendering Realism and Postmodernism* (Amsterdam: Rodopi, 2001), pp. 41–51.

Nunn, H. '*Written on the Body*: An anatomy of horror, melancholy and love', *Women: A Cultural Review* 7(1) (1996), 16–27.

O'Rourke, R. 'Fingers in the fruit basket: A feminist reading of Jeanette Winterson's *Oranges Are Not the Only Fruit*', in S. Sellers (ed.) *Feminist Criticism: Theory and Practice* (Hemel Hempstead: Harvester Wheatsheaf, 1991), pp. 57–69.

Onega, S. *Jeanette Winterson. Contemporary British Novelists* (Manchester: Manchester University Press, 2006).

Palmer, P. 'The passion: Storytelling, fantasy, desire', H. Grice and T. Woods (eds) *Postmodern Studies 25: 'I'm telling you stories': Jeanette Winterson and the Politics of Reading* (Amsterdam: Rodopi, 1998), pp. 103–116.

Palmer, P. 'Jeanette Winterson and the Lesbian postmodern', Chapter 16, in J. Acheson and S. C. E. Ross (eds.) *The Contemporary British Novel* (Edinburgh: Edinburgh University Press, 2005), pp. 189–199.

Palmer, P. 'Jeanette Winterson: Lesbian/postmodern fictions', in B. Neumeier (ed.) *Engendering Realism and Postmodernism* (Amsterdam: Rodopi, 2001), pp. 181–189.

Pearce, L. ' "Written on tablets of stone?": Jeanette Winterson, Roland Barthes, and the discourse of romantic love', in S. Raitt (ed.) *Volcanoes and Pearl Divers: Lesbian Feminist Studies* (London: Onlywomen Press, 1994), pp. 147–168.

Pearce, L. 'The emotional politics of reading', in H. Grice and T. Woods (eds) *'I'm Telling You Stories': Jeanette Winterson and the Politics of Reading* (Amsterdam: Rodopi, 1998), pp. 29–39.

Plant, S. 'The future looms: Weaving women and cybernetics', in J. Wolmark (ed.) *Cybersexualities: A Reader on Feminist Theory, Cyborgs and Cyberspace* (Edinburgh: Edinburgh University Press, 1999).

Plath, S. *The Bell Jar* (New York: Bantam, 1972).

Propp, V. *Morphology of the Folk Tale*, L.A. Wagner (ed.) and trans S. Laurence, (Austin: University of Texas Press, 1968).

Pullman, P. *His Dark Materials* (London: Scolastic Press, 1982).

Reynolds, M. and Noakes, J. *Jeanette Winterson: The Essential Guide* (London: Vintage, 2003).

Rich, A. 'Compulsory heterosexuality and Lesbian existence', in H. Abelove, M.A. Barale, and D.M. Halperin (eds) *The Lesbian and Gay Studies Reader* (New York & London: Routledge, 1993), pp. 227–254.

Rushdie, S. *Midnight's Children* (London: Picador, 1982).

Ruskin, J. *The Stones of Venice* (London: Da Capo Press, 2003).

Russo, M. *The Female Grotesque: Risk, Excess and Modernity* (New York and London: Routledge, 1994).

Schabert, I. 'Habeus Corpus 2000: The return of the body', *European Studies* 16 (2001), 87–115.

Schifferes, S. *BBC News Online*, 24 May 2002.

Seaboyer, J. 'Second death in venice: Romanticism and the compulsion to repeat in Jeanette Winterson's *The Passion*', *Contemporary Literature* 38(3) (1997), 483–509.

Shiffer, C. ' "You see, I am no stranger to love: Jeanette Winterson and the extasy of the word,' *Critique* 46(1) (Autumn 2004), 31–52.

Shklovsky, V. 'Art as technique' (first published in Russian 1917), in L.T. Lemon, and M.J. Reis (eds) and trans, *Russian Formalist Criticism: Four Essays* (Lincoln: University of Nebraska Press, 1965).

Showalter, E. 'Eternal triangles, Jeanette Winterson's *The PowerBook* is lost in cyberspace', in *The Guardian*. Saturday September 2 2000. <http://books.guardian.co.uk/reviews/generalfiction/> Accessed on 21 July 2003.

Sofia, Z. 'Virtual corporeality: A feminist view', in J. Wolmark (ed.) *Cybersexualities: A Reader on Feminist Theory, Cyborgs and Cyberspace* (Edinburgh: Edinburgh University Press, 1999).

Stein, G. *The Autobiography of Alice B. Toklas* (London: Penguin, 2001).

Stevenson, R.L. *The Strange Case of Dr Jekyll and Mr Hyde* (London: Penguin, 2004).

Stevenson, R.L. *Treasure Island* (London: Penguin, 1994).

Stimpson, C.R. 'Zero degree deviancy: The Lesbian novel in english', in E. Abel (ed.) *Writing and Sexual Difference* (Brighton: Harvester, 1982).

Stowers, C. 'Journeying with Jeanette: Transgressive travels in Winterson's fiction', in M. Maynard and J. Purvis (eds) *Hetero(sexual) Politics* (London: Taylor and Francis, 1995), pp. 139–159.

Stowers, C. ' "No legitimate place, no land, no fatherland": Communities of women in the fiction of Roberts and Winterson', *Critical Survey* 8(1) (1996), 69–79.

Swift, G. *Waterland* (London: Picador, 1996).

Taylor, P. '*The PowerBook* needs a new hard drive', *The Independent*, 21 May 2002.

Tew, P. 'Wintersonian masculinities', in S. Andermahr (ed.) *Jeanette Winterson: A Contemporary Critical Guide* (London: Continuum, 2007), pp. 114–129.

Thorne, M. 'Satire and SF meet – on another planet' *The Independent on Sunday*, 12 October 2007. http://arts.independent.co.uk/books/reviews/article3050454.ece Accessed on 6 January 2008.

Tolkein, J.R.R. *The Lord of the Rings* (London: Harper Collins, 1993).

Trumbach, R. 'Sodomitical subcultures, sodomitical roles, and the gender revolution of the eighteenth century: The recent historiography', in R.P. Maccubin (ed.) *'Tis Nature's Fault* (Cambridge: Cambridge University Press, 1987).

Walter, N. *The Independent*, 19 September, 1992.

Ward, E. *A Compleat and Humorous Account of All the Remarkable Clubs and Societies in the Cities of London and Westminster* 7th edition (London: J. Wren, 1756).

Waugh, P. *Practising Postmodernism/Reading Modernism* (London: Hodder Arnold, 1992).

Wingfield, R. 'Lesbian writers in the mainstream: Sara Maitland, Jeanette Winterson and Emma Donoghue', in E. Hutton (ed.) *Beyond Sex and Romance: The Politics of Contemporary Lesbian Fiction* (London: Women's Press, 1998), pp. 60–80.

Wittig, M. *Les Guerillères* (New York: Avon, 1973).

Wittig, M. 'One is not born a woman', in *The Straight Mind and Other Essays* (Boston: Beacon Press, 1992), pp. 9–20.

Woolf, V. *A Room of One's Own* (London: Granada, 1981).

Woolf, V. *Orlando* (Oxford: Oxford University Press, 1992).

Woolf, V. 'Professions for women', in M. Barrett (ed.) *Virginia Woolf: Women and Writing* (London: The Women's Press, 1992).

Woolf, V. *To the Lighthouse* (London: Penguin, 2000a).

Woolf, V. *The Waves* (London: Penguin, 2000b).

Zimmerman, B. 'Exiting from patriarchy: The Lesbian novel of development', in E. Abel, M. Hirsch, and E. Langland (eds) *The Voyage In: Fictions of Female Development* (Hanover, NH: University Press of New England, 1983).

Zimmerman, B. 'Lesbians like this and like that', in S. Munt (ed.) *New Lesbian Criticism* (Hemel Hempstead: Harvester Wheatsheaf, 1992), pp. 1–15.

Zimmerman, B. 'What has never been: Lesbian literary criticism in the 1980s,' in E. Showalter (ed.) *The New Feminist Criticism* (London: Virago, 1986), pp. 200–224.

INDEX